The Five Wealth Currencies

A Holistic Journey From
Welfare To Millionaire

Njeri Gichia-Broussard, MBA

ISBN: 979-8-9918393-0-3

Author Contact Info

Njeri Gichia-Broussard

407-279-1562

Njeri@lighthouse.coach

https://lighthouse.coach/

Dedication

To my sons, Isaiah and Matthew. May I leave you a foundation to build generational wealth in all its currencies for generations to come in the "hyphen" family. Know that Mommy loves you and will always be with you.

Introduction

I left home at 17 years old in June of 1992 with a net worth of ZERO DOLLARS. But I did have a full academic scholarship to study chemical engineering at Florida A&M University (FAMU), in Tallahassee, FL. The scholarship was sponsored by the Monsanto Company. The company also provided me with paid internships every summer until I graduated, contingent upon my maintaining certain academic standards and progress. I also had enough Delta Airlines frequent flier miles (from our family trips to Kenya over the years) for a free round-trip ticket to New York to visit my family when desired.

Within my first week at FAMU, I volunteered to be on the campus SAFE team, which would escort students across campus at night. I kept hearing about this guy from Los Angeles who was an architecture student. The buzz caught my attention. When I somehow *saw* his name on a piece of paper, I knew he was going to be my husband. And that was before I met him! No kidding. We finally met, and I couldn't fight the chemistry between us. That chemistry led to marriage. Because he is a fundamentalist Muslim, we initially were in a Mut'ah, or temporary marriage. When I became pregnant at 19, we entered a Nikah, or permanent marriage.

Romance changes. When ours did, my son's father left our marriage and chose not to pay child support. I supported us through Aid to Families with Dependent Children, Welfare for Women, Infants, and Children (WIC) and food stamps. President Bill Clinton had signed the Welfare-to-Work Act during that time, so I had one year from the divorce decree date to figure out how to take care of myself and my two-year-old son while finishing school.

When the divorce was finalized in 1997, I was left with over $40,000 ($78,142.80 in 2024 inflation-adjusted dollars) in student loans (both his and mine because I co-signed his student loans), credit card debt and medical debt. I had no idea what I was going to do. Welfare and any form of public assistance I could get wasn't a feasible solution for me.

How did I go from welfare to millionaire over the last 25 or so years? That is a good question that I intend to answer in this book. I will also give you insight on how romantic relationships directly affect your net wealth.

In my case, I went from a marital relationship that left me on welfare to one where my current husband, Darryl, and I have a net worth of over two million dollars on any given day in the stock market. Darryl and I met while he was living in Orlando and I was living in New Orleans. We were introduced -interestingly - at a mutual friend's wedding in Auckland, New Zealand. He was engaged to someone else at the time, and I was dating other people, but we seemed to have an instant connection. He married and divorced her within two years after we met. The ink wasn't even dry on his divorce papers when he reached out to our mutual friend to get my contact information. I didn't understand why he was calling so I simply treated him as a friend. After three months of long-distance communicating with my friend, during one of our conversations, I told him I still wasn't dating anyone.

He then informed me, "I'm dating you."

I replied, "Oh. Well, if that's the case, then I need to see all three of your credit reports and FICO scores."

He thought I was joking. I made it clear that there was no point in us dating if our financials didn't match – because I was no longer dating for any other reason than marriage. He went to a New Orleans Saints game with our mutual friend the Sunday after that announcement. He told him what I said. Our mutual friend laughed and said, "Yeah, that sounds like Njeri!"

Long story short, he came back to me and said, "I'll show you mine if you show me yours." And just like that, we got financially naked long before we were physically naked.

Thanks to our prenuptial agreement, independently I have one million dollars in investible assets - excluding my primary residence. In the United States this makes me a high net worth individual and accredited investor. As of this writing (in 2024), I have never earned six figures in Social Security taxable income in a year as an individual.

I started out as the youngest child of two upper-middle-class parents who were both first-generation college graduates; my mother was Black American from western North Carolina, and my father was an immigrant from Kenya. My mother worked part-time cleaning houses for White folks and in the college dorms to pay the expenses outside of her small academic scholarship to Warren Wilson College. My father was chosen to come to the United States to study chemistry as part of the Kennedy Airlifts. The airlifts were the idea of an innovate young leader from Kenya, Tom Mboya, who sought to have intelligent Kenyan students brought to America for higher education. His efforts led him to then Senator John F. Kennedy, who sponsored an impressive number of travel and education scholarships for these African students, with my father being one of them. He arrived on the same plane as future President Barack Obama's father.

Both my parents grew up in poverty, so I grew up learning to be extremely frugal. When I announced that I was going to pivot from engineering to become a financial advisor, my oldest sister said she wasn't surprised. She shared a story of a trip to the grocery store with her and my mother when I was five. My mother was putting the groceries on the belt to pay when I asked her, "Is that a good deal?" My mother doesn't remember this incident, but when she asked my older sister (who is 10 plus years my senior), she said it was 1979. While she also didn't hear me ask the question, a woman behind them in line did. Impressed, she pointed out my unusual financial acumen to my mother.

I have built the bulk of my financial wealth through investing in the stock market after studying chemical engineering for six years. I have made multiple mistakes along the way. Mistakes like waiting to invest in my 401k, borrowing from my 401k, ignoring collections debt, signing up for high-interest credit cards and then running up debt to the card limits, then only paying the minimum required, co-signing my ex-husband's loans even though I knew he was bad with money, and waiting too long to get into real estate. I made career mistakes too that impacted my income while working in Corporate America. I didn't make wise health decisions, and that has significantly affected all my other wealth currencies over the years.

Yes, there are multiple wealth currencies, and they may not be what you think they are – so it's a great thing that you are willing to employ what you will learn in this tool. The wealth currencies we will investigate, despite my missteps along the way, have led to my financial success.

Chapter 1

The Currency Understanding

"Money won't create success, the freedom to make it will." **Nelson Mandela, South African Activist and Statesman**

When most of us think of wealth, we think of currency, specifically financial currency – MONEY! Money is, in fact, perhaps the most well-known and coveted form of currency globally. Whether it's the most important is arguable.

What should we understand about the most popular form of currency? The dollar, the pound, the euro, the peso, the yen, or the term for it in your part of the world? Currency is a commonly used monetary system that is usually issued by a government and used in an economy to support investment, trade, and the appraisal of goods and services. Money performs several crucial tasks.

A tangible medium of exchange, currency eases transactions and eliminates the necessity for a barter system in the exchange of goods and services. While barter is still a currency in some regions, many find the practice can be inequitable and not produce the tangible need to provide a stated investment in return for a defined object, good, or service. In that same vein, money offers a common way to measure value, which makes it possible to price products and services consistently. Although the value of currency is subject to fluctuations due to inflation, interest rates, economic growth, geopolitical stability, and other economic variables, it's possible to save and retrieve it in the future. Money currency can also be used to pay debts and make future payments possible in the form of credit or loans, which is a money task that leads many into trouble. There are two primary types of modern currencies:

- Physical Currency: Coins and paper money that can be handled and traded in person, such as banknotes.
- Digital Currency: Any kind of money that exists in a digital format and is transmitted electronically, including bank deposits, cryptocurrency, and digital wallets. Digital currency has become highly popular, with some cryptocurrency founders facing legal and other backlash for shoddy dealings.

The abundance of priceless resources or material belongings is known as wealth. Writer Alan Watts wrote, ***"There are a great many people accumulating what they think is vast wealth, but it's only money."*** Wealth and money, obviously, in Watts' opinion, are not the same thing. And that can be true, depending on what you believe is genuine wealth and what types of currency encourages, promotes, and supports what makes you wealthy.

When we consider financial currency, we should also understand that it includes a broad spectrum of resources and assets that can support the prosperity and financial stability of an individual, business, or other entity. Some of the metrics used to quantify wealth include financial assets such as bonds, equities, and other liquid assets. Other areas include real estate, natural resources, personal property, business ownership and intellectual property.

Combined, these areas encompass home and industrial properties, land, agriculture, minerals, oils and related, jewels, cars, collectibles, antiques, business ownership or stock ownership. It also includes patents, trademarks, copyrights, and other intellectual properties that generate income. Wealth is also accumulated and distributed through specific categories like private, corporate, and national wealth.

Being wealthy, financially secure, or rich are times we have often heard as things to aspire to. And why not? Wealth provides economic security, investment potential, an increased standard of living, and increased aspirations and opportunities for power and influence. One's net worth, your financial gold number, after your debts and money obligations are attended to, is a common way to quantify wealth. A solid net worth has the power to affect both personal prospects and, more general society dynamics.

Money wealth is, again, only one currency that should mark the profitability evident in our lives. There are other currencies that govern our lives and determine the true definition and evidence of wealth for each of us.

"The definition of wealth depends on who you ask. Some people say wealth is purely monetary, it's what money can buy. Others believe it goes well beyond cash in the bank and has mostly to do with feelings of freedom and flexibility.

The bottom line? There's no one correct definition of wealth, and you need to decide what it means for you. And according to financial advisors, how people define wealth often changes throughout their lives." E. Napoletano, **How To Define What Wealth Means To You, Forbes.com (July 2023)**

My life journey taught me about wealth, the presence of it, the absence of it, and the varying emotions that attach themselves to wealth. That journey revealed that there are several areas of life that not only demand we be healthy and wise but also directly impact our financial wealth. When your currency in key life areas is not addressed, nurtured, and charged properly, it will hamper your ability to increase your net worth and cash flow. Since financial wealth is a vibrant, blinking billboard over our lives, it's important that we fully understand the weightier currencies at work daily. Think of currencies as fluids in a body of wealth.

The currencies I am talking about are:

- Financial: Net worth, which again is basically financial assets minus financial debts. I learned about the accumulation of financial wealth in the book *The Millionaire Next Door* and discovered a new formula to incorporate into financial wealth: your accumulator of wealth score. This is now how I measure my wealth even though I have never inherited anything except a reservation plot in my maternal grandparents' church graveyard in Arden, NC.

- Knowledge: This currency hadn't occurred to me until I was talking about what was then only four wealth currencies to a whole life insurance client. That client, Braxton Skinner, asked me, "What about knowledge currency?" A light bulb went off in my head, and it changed everything. He explained that when I presented the wealth currencies to him and his wife, he thought to himself, "So what's the ask?" He had already told a mutual associate of ours (who is a life insurance agent and financial advisor) that he thought life insurance (especially whole life insurance) was a total fraud. I told him I understood and showed him my and my husband's net worth. He remarked to his wife, "Look, they have TWO commas in their net worth!" He also noted that no other financial advisor had been so transparent about their finances. Since we're both from the same hometown, he realized that I had a knowledge of wealth beyond the survival state he and his wife were living in, and it helped me realize that knowledge is a valuable currency.

- Social: Social wealth was a major factor in my time in Corporate America. I distinctly remember being at work one day and realizing I had gained influence through my relationships with White and Black people at the plant. I had to consider, *"Now, what am I going to DO with this influence?"* That was the summer of 2004 when I stopped getting chemical relaxers and started wearing extensions to grow my natural hair. This was virtually unheard of since, in Corporate America, Black women didn't wear their naturally textured hair in twists, coils, or curls. We were subtly trained to style our hair like the highest-positioned Black woman in the company. I've never gone back to chemically treated hair styles, but I have used my social influence to increase my overall wealth. I met my current husband, who is a MASTER at social wealth (being the New Orleanian that he is) shortly after that. Much of my social wealth today is due to my relationship with him.

- Health: You would think having laparoscopic surgery for my gallbladder six months after my first child was born would wake me up to health as a currency, and it did. I was nearly financially bankrupted from the medical bills. Health wealth never became clearer to

5

me than when I started having seizures in October 2020. The diagnosis and treatment options again opened my eyes to how health as a currency is critical to sustaining life itself.

- Time: My first recollection of time wealth comes from the song "Dust In The Wind" by Kansas. My seventh-grade teacher, Ms. Grimm, played it for us, and one line is burned in my mind, "And all your money won't another minute buy." Our time should not only be spent wisely but productively on achieving goals and enjoying every moment of life with which we're gifted.
- Spiritual: While I am still learning about the value of spiritual wealth, it's critical to each of the other currencies we will continue to explore. Spiritual currency relates to having faith in something (or someone) larger than the life that we can see before us. Each of us must find a way to obtain spiritual wealth. My spiritual currency is not yet as astute as my other wealth currency experiences, but I'm continuing to delve into it, intrigued by the glimpses of its importance.

As a wealth coach, clearly my role and desire is to help you make intelligent, wise, profitable financial decisions that will not only increase your current net worth but also help you intentionally create a strong financial legacy for your family. Yet, as someone who has felt the downside of not having sufficient revenue and lived the upside of making knowledgeable money choices and properly increasing my assets, I also know that the other currencies have contributed to a fuller, holistically wealthy life.

Currency by currency we will explore the key points you need to capitalize your wealth.

Chapter 2

Financial Wealth

Our approach to money, including planning ahead and delaying gratification, is set by age seven. That startling piece of information is according to research released in 2013 by behavior experts David Whitebread and Sue Bingham of the University of Cambridge. Get that, at the age of seven! The funny thing is one of the reasons I'm financially wealthy now is because of the stock my father bought for me for Christmas in 1981 when I was about 7 years old. Each of my three older sisters also received a stock present based on the principles of investment he'd learned, probably from the White men at work. Those two main principles at the time:

1. Invest in companies you will use.
2. Invest in tech stocks when you can afford it and can stomach the risk.

He bought my oldest sister stock in General Motors (GM) because she was about to get her driver's license (you had to be 18 in New Jersey, but we had moved to Florida, which allowed a learner's permit at 15). He bought my second sister stock in Disney because we lived in Jacksonville, FL, and Epcot had just opened at Disney World in nearby Orlando, FL. He thought Disney stock would take off as a result. He bought my third sister stock in Wendy's (just before the "Where's the beef?" '80s marketing campaign). And he bought me stock in a little computer company you may have heard of called Apple, because my father thought computers were the future. This was largely based on information from his nephew studying Computer Science in France (that cousin later came to live with us and taught me basic computer coding). He also paid the hefty price tag for an Apple IIe computer when it first came out. Now, you might be thinking, "Heck yeah! A share of Apple bought in 1981 valued over 40 years later...that must be worth millions of dollars today!" Well, no, it's not.

Even with the stock splits over the years and increases in the stock price and market cap, the millions assumption doesn't apply to me. My dad sold the stock to pay for a family trip to Kenya at some point (a social wealth investment). I did get a couple of dividend checks from Apple through my Dean Witter Reynolds Brokerage account. The financial education and feeling of empowerment that I got from owning a company was priceless (like Mastercard PRICELESS)! You see, after my dad gave me the stock, he showed me how to check on its performance every day in the Wall Street Journal. He taught me about P/E (price-to-earnings) ratios and dividends, and I developed a burning desire to obtain a Master of Business Administration (MBA) degree.

The White male hippies of the '60s had become the White male yuppies of the '80s, and they ruled Wall Street. From what my child's brain could gather, that also meant they controlled the country. Getting an MBA and learning how to invest seemed to be the way to financial wealth, so I was focused on learning that from White men. My observations at the time weren't that far off based on news reports, and Dad and I consumed those reports. He was a news junkie reading the *New York Times, Wall Street Journal, Florida Times Union,* and *Jacksonville Journal* regularly. When the video cassette recorder (VCR) came out, he installed one on each television so he could record the evening news on the other two big three stations while we watched CBS with Dan Rather. Then, at 7 pm, he would watch the MacNeill/Lehrer NewsHour on PBS.

My parents tried to start their own business, a hair salon named Mandeleo. My mother even convinced me to get a Jheri curl, a wet, bouncy, curly style that was popular at the time. The hair style was her Christmas gift to me in 1982. My siblings and I worked to market the business. I will never forget we were passing out flyers advertising the business on April 1, 1984, when we heard the tragic news that R&B superstar Marvin Gaye was shot by his father. My mother loved Marvin Gaye, and I'll never forget watching him perform the national anthem at the NBA All-Star Game in 1983. Their business failed within three years because they were both working full-time jobs and weren't there to supervise the hair stylists who were stealing from my parents left and right. I learned then that **owning a business and running a business are two VASTLY different things**.

My parents weren't ones to give an allowance for chores around the house. If you wanted money (outside of the tooth fairy and birthday money), you had to get a job. I had to buy my own yearbooks and pay for my own entertainment once I started my menstrual cycle. They taught us to be incredibly frugal. That included all these things (and these are just a few examples):

9

- We didn't throw any food away...EVER! We were expected to eat leftovers until they were gone.
- We purchased off-brand as often as possible.
- My mother made our clothes well into the '80s. She even made extra money as a seamstress when not working her full-time job.
- Always use as little toilet paper as possible. My mother and I argued about this, ESPECIALLY when I started my menstrual cycle. Some frugal habits DON'T transfer down through the generations.
- Push the trash down in the trash bag to maximize the use of the plastic bag.
- Set the A/C higher during the day when no one is home, and at night while people are sleeping, use ceiling fans.
- If it's not in use, turn it off.
- Don't waste water (turn off the faucet while you brush your teeth).
- Hang clothes out to dry on the clothesline in the backyard. Only use the dryer when it rains.
- Buying new clothes regularly is not necessary. I wore hand-me-down clothes until I was about eight years old.
- Use the furniture you have until you can't. I slept in bed with one of my sisters until we moved to Florida when I was five and got my own bed.

My first regular-paying job was as a neighborhood babysitter, starting at about 13 or 14 years old in the summer of 1988. I got the job through social wealth, as my older sister had grown tired of babysitting for the family. She'd become more serious about focusing on dating instead of studying to complete her degree after she ran into her high school sweetheart, even though our parents demanded academic excellence.

I was paid $10 for the evening, starting at 7 pm, until the parents came home to their three sons. I did that for a couple of years and got irritated when I didn't get a raise or wasn't paid more when the parents stayed out later than normal. I stopped working for them, and I got my first tax-paying job at 16 years old, in the summer of 1991, at the brand-new Popeye's fast-food chain on San Jose. It was ideal for me because it was right up the road from our home.

My dad didn't believe I would apply for a job at the chain, but I walked up there, put in an application to be a cashier, and came home with a job the same afternoon. My parents were very impressed with me. One of the few things I remember my father saying to me early in high school was, "If you're going to college, you better get a scholarship because we're not paying for it." That statement and the benefit of my being much younger than my older sisters gave me the benefit of the wisdom of their experiences (knowledge wealth) without having to go through it myself (time wealth). So, I studied hard and took advanced placement and dual enrollment classes in high school to minimize how much time and tuition I would spend in college. But most important was my major and how I chose it.

You see, my mother was a nurse midwife who, at the time, was working on her PhD in Nursing at the University of Florida in Gainesville. Her doctoral thesis was titled *Mothers And Others: Afro-American Women's Descriptions of Motherhood (African-American)*. She was their first black candidate and a McKnight Fellow. My father was a United States patent-holding research chemist working for Revlon Cosmetics.

11

At first, I wanted to be a veterinarian. I loved animals, and being a doctor was an acceptable career for my very conservative parents, who had such high standards for their children. Then, one night, when my second sister and I were stopped at a gas station on Philips Highway, I saw a cat limping after it had been hit by a car. It was bloody and battered with one eye hanging out. It was then that I realized that all the animals I was going to treat weren't going to be healthy, so I changed my focus.

My father's specialty was as a research chemist for hair products with Revlon. I loved hair and thought, *"I'll be a chemist like him!"* When I told him I wanted to be a research chemist like him, he told me, "Be a chemical engineer. They make more money!"

I didn't know what a chemical engineer did, so I asked my AP Chemistry teacher Mr. Otto Phanstiel (a former chemical engineer), "What does an engineer do?" He told me, "They solve problems!" I liked puzzles and solving problems, so I thought it might be a good fit.

Having landed on being an engineer, I knew I needed to do well on standardized tests to qualify for academic scholarships, so I studied, and studied, and studied. My father signed me up for standardized test preparation classes (and actually paid for them, which was out of character for them). My parents had previously paid for standardized test preparation classes for my second and third sisters. It wasn't until they got into a car accident and my parents looked at the police report that they realized my sisters had skipped class to take a boy home. This motivated me to really stay focused on the test preparation classes. I knocked it out of the park on my National Merit Scholars test and ended up as a National Achievement Scholar and a National Merit Finalist. I had scholarships pouring in from all over the country, inviting me to attend various colleges and universities. Still, I was undecided.

I had narrowed it down to Harvard and Florida A&M University (FAMU), but it was hard to decide. At Harvard I wouldn't have to choose a major right away, but it was only a partial scholarship, and I would have to work and go to school or else use student loans. I had learned from watching my older sisters deal with student loans that borrowing wasn't the way I wanted to go. I had also watched them work full-time while going to school (living at home with a curfew AND paying my parents rent). I knew that was out of the question for me. Even at that young age, I knew I needed to be free from control. I needed the freedom promised in the United States Constitution. I needed the freedom with which White men seemed to have been born with in this country. I wanted financial independence and freedom to control my time.

I made my choice when I attended an after-party following the Florida Classic Football game, a huge Florida rivalry game between then Bethune Cookman College (BCC, a historically Black college in Daytona Beach, FL) and FAMU. I was invited by the then FAMU President, Dr. Frederick Humphries, to attend an interest session for prospective students. He had each of the students fill out an interest form with their grade point average and SAT score and put it in a box. He then started speaking about FAMU and its history. He was moving with his words. Then he started pulling interest forms out of the box: "So and so, if you choose FAMU, you get a full scholarship!" and he went on like that. One after the other. Then he got to a name he couldn't pronounce, "I'm not sure how to say this name. Njeri. Gichia. You get the Cadillac of scholarships! Full tuition, room, board, books, fees, a living stipend, and a paid internship every summer sponsored by a Fortune 500 company!" I was taken aback!

Harvard was Harvard. But FAMU was an HBCU, and I didn't really know what it meant to be Black. I had grown up in a predominantly White neighborhood in Jacksonville, FL, with

13

few (if any) Black American friends. All I knew of HBCUs was Edward Waters College in Jacksonville (the oldest HBCU in the country). That school wasn't accredited, so I did some homework. If I studied for my bachelor's degree in chemical engineering at FAMU, my degree would be from FAMU, but the upper-level engineering classes would be taught at the FAMU/FSU College of Engineering. That engineering school was accredited, so I would be okay to go there. I chose FAMU.

The FAMU Years

Shortly before I graduated from Stanton College Preparatory School with my high school diploma on June 1, 1992, I got a call from the Life Gets Better (LGB) scholarship coordinator, Debra Williams-Hardy (now Chappell) at FAMU. The LGB scholarship was (as FAMU's president Humphries said) THE Cadillac of scholarships, and she was calling to let me know which Fortune 500 company would be sponsoring me.

"Monsanto," she said, and in line with my request to intern the first summer before starting at FAMU, I would be completing a summer internship at their plant in Pensacola, FL. I had never heard of the company before, so when I told my parents, my dad exclaimed, "That's a good company!"

A couple of weeks after graduation, we packed up my belongings in the family minivan. Because I was still only 17, I couldn't rent an apartment, but the human resources contact at the plant helped me secure housing on the nearby University of West Florida (UWF) campus in a co-ed dorm, much to my parents' displeasure as FAMU had separate male and female dorms.

Monday, June 22, 1992, was my first day of work as a chemical engineering intern at the Pensacola Monsanto plant. They manufactured Nylon 66 carpet fiber for Monsanto wear dated carpet, as well as tire yarn for car tires. I reported to a White female PhD in the research and development department. I was paid $625 ($1,401.19 in 2024 inflation-adjusted dollars) every two weeks as a salaried employee with a pension. That works out to $7.81/hour ($17.51/hour in 2024 inflation-adjusted dollars). The minimum wage in 1992 was $4.25/hour ($9.53/hour in 2024 inflation-adjusted dollars), so I was elated with my compensation. As an intern I completed wicking studies and research on the effects of carpet finishes on plastics via absorption. I was on top of the world! I wanted to make a good impression, so I even worked overtime without being asked in an attempt to finish all the assignments I had been given. This was before I learned about the tactic of a manager giving more work than an employee could possibly finish just to see what the employee would do. I was responsible for my own meals, my own shopping, my own laundry, and my own bookkeeping. I paid my own rent and car insurance. I was, for the most part, a fully functioning adult at the end of the six weeks. I then moved to Tallahassee to start my freshman year at FAMU.

As I have mentioned previously, my Life Gets Better Scholarship covered all tuition, books, fees, room, and board and included a spending stipend each semester. The conditions were that my grade point average had to stay above 3.0 cumulative, and I had to be enrolled in a minimum of 12 credit hours each semester (Spring and Fall) to be considered a full-time scholarship student. While I had completed over 30 hours of transferable credits through my high school's dual enrollment and advanced placement program, I wanted to be certain that I was secure in my knowledge of the chemical engineering basics. With that in mind, I decided to take General Chemistry I and Calculus I as part of my fall 1992 course load, even though I had passed both advanced placement exams with scores of 3 and 4, respectively.

When I arrived on campus, I was overwhelmed by the number of credit cards I could get. And to be able to get a free T-shirt for completing the application seemed like a good idea at the time. Against my better judgment, I signed up for them without reading the fine print, which was against two critical principles my mother always mentioned to me when I was growing up:

- Read everything before you sign it.
- Read the fine print.

On the other hand, because I had three older sisters who had lived at home until they married as twenty-something-year-old adults, I learned a thing or two from their experiences with credit cards. So even though every weekend I was charging shopping trips at the music store like a crackhead running up a drug tab, I was paying my credit card balance in full every month, but I was also not saving or investing; that was a BIG financial wealth mistake. I also took a job on campus working for the SAFE team, which was the campus escort service. Students (especially females) could call us, and we'd send someone trained in self-defense to escort the student across campus at night. I learned self-defense and was a receptionist at the call center in the student union from 7 pm to midnight. When things were slow, I would study. I ended my first semester with a 3.8 grade point average (straight As with a B in English just because the professor didn't like me and I missed one class). I wasn't satisfied, and neither was my father (his standard was the Dean's List). During winter break, I got a job wrapping gifts at the Jacksonville Landing Mall. I thought about my father's dissatisfaction as I filled a need to earn money so I could maintain as much independence as possible.

As I thought about my father's dissatisfaction, I knew I needed to study and do more to make the Dean's list. So, in my second semester (which was Spring 1993), I went hard and decided to really focus on school. I started out with 19 credit hours, including a Fortran computer code class. I ended the semester with a 4.0 grade point average after withdrawing from the three-credit hour Fortran class. The 19-hour load was too much while working at night on the SAFE team. With 16 additional credit hours on my transcript, I was elated. This set the stage for how I started my second summer internship in Pensacola with Monsanto.

I returned to the plant and was again reporting to the same woman. She had specifically requested me because I did such a great job the first summer. Because Monsanto was a pay for performance company, I got a pay raise thanks to the transferred and completed credit hours from my freshman year. In the summer of 1993, I was paid $1500 every two weeks or $18.75/ hour ($3,265.12 every two weeks [$40.81/hour in 2024 inflation-adjusted dollars]) as a salaried chemical engineering intern employee with a pension. Again, I was still responsible for my own financial and other responsibilities since I had left home a year earlier, and this year, I was planning to live off the University of West Florida's campus in a 2-bedroom apartment with a roommate.

At the time, my mother needed a new vehicle, and I needed a way to get to and from work again for the summer. So, in May 1993, I negotiated with my parents to buy my mother's 1987 Mitsubishi Galant from them for the Kelly Blue Book value of $2800 ($6,094.89 in 2024 inflation-adjusted dollars) and pay for my own portion of the car insurance cost to my parents while continuing to be carried on their car insurance plan. This was my first car purchase, at just 18 years old. I knew nothing about car loans and, at that time, was paying my credit card off every month.

I set up a payment plan with my parents and went back for a full 12 weeks of summer internship.

I managed to finish sophomore year with not as high of a grade point average after starting my first upper-level chemical engineering class. Nonetheless, Monsanto kept their word on pay for performance by increasing pay based on a range of credit hours acquired. I returned to the Pensacola Monsanto plant in the summer of 1994 and spent 12 weeks there working for a White male PhD. I was paid $1666.20 every two weeks or $20.83/hour ($3,536.35/two weeks or $44.21/hour in 2024 inflation-adjusted dollars).

Memorial Day weekend of that year, on my way back to Pensacola from Tallahassee after visiting my boyfriend from the SAFE Team, I attempted suicide. I was anxious and beyond depressed at the thought of us breaking up. I set the car on cruise control at 75 mph, closed my eyes and let go of the steering wheel. The 1987 Galant hit an overpass column and flipped three times. The emergency responders had to cut the roof off the car to get me out. The car was totaled. As a result, I suffer from chronic neck and back pain (health wealth).

It was social wealth that kept me able to get to and from work for the rest of the summer, and I was about to learn a lot about how wealth currencies interact when exchanged. You see, at the end of the summer internship in 1994, I made a life-changing decision. I chose life when I got a positive pregnancy test after a late summer visit from my boyfriend.

Choosing to give birth to, keep, and personally raise my son was a significant financial decision. That decision and (Florida abortion laws expiring) left my father with the question, "So when are you getting married?" While it took several months and a growing belly for me to say yes, **I believe who you marry and/or procreate with are the most significant financial**

18

decisions one can make in life. It has been documented in research studies that finances are one of the top reasons married couples divorce. So, in less than six months, at the end of 1994, I made two life-changing decisions: to keep my baby and marry my son's father.

When I informed my scholarship coordinator of my condition, she reminded me of the conditions of my scholarship. I wasn't performing well in my chemical engineering classes, so my grade point average was going down each semester even though I was still maintaining a high enough grade point average to maintain my scholarship. When I informed my Monsanto company representative, he told me to take the summer off in 1995 as maternity leave since the baby was born in mid-April, and I would have course finals I would need to go back and complete anyway.

So, in the summer of 1995, I stayed at home with my baby for as long as my brain, body, and checking account would allow. Then, I got a job as an administrative assistant through a temporary employment (temp) agency, earning $6.00/hour ($12.38 / hour in 2024 inflation-adjusted dollars) working during the day. My new husband continued his night shift job at McDonald's at minimum wage. I had moved in with him on one side of a duplex in a seedy part of Tallahassee. The owner was a slumlord and had a housing authority tenant on the other side. The yard was supposed to have grass, but there was only dirt in the front. The structure hadn't been properly maintained and was infested with German roaches. We had little to no furniture, and our version of a sofa was three large cushions on the floor. We were so poor that our wedding gift from the drug-dealing neighbor was a used twin mattress he'd found somewhere. He gave it to my husband, and that was an upgrade from the egg cushion mattress cover we were using as a bed on the floor.

When the fall of 1995 started, I was grateful to be on scholarship but barely could afford food and other necessities on my stipend. Daycare was out of the question from a cost perspective, so my husband and I arranged our class schedules such that one of us was always with our son while the other was in class. And while alternating custody during class changes left no time for studying, it did solve our childcare problem. The only problem it yielded was low grades for both of us when our transcripts came out. It didn't help that as soon as we married on December 20, 1994, my mother asked for a copy of our marriage certificate. She said it was for the family tree project. I later discovered it was so she could remove me from their car insurance and lower their out-of-pocket cost since I totaled the car under their insurance, all while they kept the insurance payout for the vehicle even though I had completed my payment plan to them for the car. In addition to that my husband's grades were so low he no longer qualified for financial aid, so I took out a student loan with my good credit to cover his tuition, books, and fees. I had also added him as an authorized user to my credit cards since his credit was trash. In the fall of 1995, I was hit with another financial strain when I had gallbladder surgery with no health insurance. I ended up with a $20,000 medical bill ($41,278.22 in 2024 inflation-adjusted dollars). Then, in the spring of 1996, I started to see things about my husband that were going to affect my financial wealth even more clearly than I had ever seen them before, but I will dig into that in the social wealth section.

One positive financial decision I made while living with my first husband was to **purchase renter's insurance**. We had a flood in our duplex, and it damaged much of our property and the old carpet in the unit. I took that as an opportunity to negotiate getting new carpet in the unit and to get new furniture with the insurance payout.

In the summer of 1996, I resumed my internship program with Monsanto at their Carondelet plant in St. Louis, MO and brought my husband and son with me. I had requested to work at the corporate office, but this was the closest my corporate contact could get me. I was paid $7,748 for the summer, which worked out to $1549.60 every two weeks and $19.37/hour when minimum wage was $4.75/hour (2024 inflation-adjusted dollars for each are: $15,532.54 for the summer, $3,106.51 every two weeks, and $38.83/hour with minimum wage at $9.52/hour). One of my sister's husbands had a used vehicle he was willing to loan me to get back and forth to work. I had been with the company so long they didn't even do a performance review with me at the end of the summer. But perhaps that's because my life was falling apart. On August 2, 1996, I came home from work at Monsanto in St. Louis and found one of the most financially devastating notes anyone can ever find. It was a "Dear John" letter from my husband. He'd left and taken our son to his father's place in Los Angeles. I had to learn the legal system at the young age of 21 and very quickly.

In mid-August of 1996, I returned to Tallahassee, FL, without my son to hopefully complete my final year of studies as a Bachelor of Science degree candidate in chemical engineering at FAMU, all while my personal life looked like a snow globe that had been shaken. My world was turned upside down. I was going through a divorce, failing in school, but killing it on my internships. Financially, my world was falling apart.

At first, I was racking up credit card debt, trying to pay for a divorce attorney to try to regain physical custody of my 16-month-old son. Thankfully, my income was low enough to qualify for a pro bono divorce attorney after I qualified for food stamps. My grades weren't good, but I was in survival mode and didn't know what else to do. I went through the fall of 1996 and spring of 1997, still on scholarship but on academic probation. This affected my financial and health wealth significantly.

While I wasn't doing well in school, Monsanto Chemical Company was impressed enough with my performance as a chemical engineering intern that they offered me a fifth internship for the summer of 1997. There was only one catch...it was going to be in Muscatine, IA. The divorce in progress was messy and taking its toll on my health and finances. I had sunk to selling my plasma periodically to make ends meet. I knew a job with Monsanto was going to pay more than any temporary job I could get over the summer in Tallahassee...so I took it. I was to be paid $10,016 for 13 weeks, which equates to $1540.92 every two weeks and $19.26/hour (or $19,628.86 for 13 weeks, $3,019.82 every two weeks, and $ 37.74/hour in 2024 inflation-adjusted dollars). I was desperate for income and space from my soon-to-be ex-husband, so I took the job and my son and I headed to Iowa. My soon-to-be ex-husband wasn't happy about it, but I had been granted full custody while the divorce was in progress.

I rented a small part of a duplex on the corner of 4th and Iowa in downtown Muscatine. I was still driving the car my brother-in-law loaned me, but I irresponsibly ignored the oil leak, and partway into the summer, the engine seized up while I was in a rural area of Iowa. I had the car towed and got an estimate for repairs. The mechanic told me it would cost more to repair the car than it was worth. I managed to get a rental car on my credit card even though I wasn't 25 years old yet. I drove the rental car for four weeks while I argued with my sister about who should pay for the car since the oil leak was already in existence when I got the car. Eventually, my brother-in-law and I agreed to split the Kelly Blue Book value, I paid him, and we called it a done deal. I got a ride to and from the babysitter and work for the rest of the summer from a neighboring intern who was sweet on me (social wealth) and worked at the plant.

At the end of the summer of 1997, I received an offer for full-time employment as a chemical engineer with the Monsanto company at $46,000/yr as a salaried employee at the Muscatine location. I went back to Tallahassee to do my 6th (and what I hoped would be final) year as a BS in Chemical Engineering candidate. I struggled. My divorce was finalized on September 24, 1997. I was granted full custody with my ex-husband having liberal visitation with our son and was required to pay $250/month in child support ($489.94/month in 2024 inflation-adjusted dollars). I was drowning in debt, and because of President Bill Clinton signing the Welfare Reform Act, which limited welfare recipients to one year of benefits before being forced to work, I knew I needed to get a full-time job. I had no car, which made getting back and forth to class extremely difficult, and I was racking up nothing but debt. Because my grades were so low, I was dropped from the Life Gets Better Scholarship program and had to take out student loans to sustain myself while I raised my son. I got no child support from my ex-husband after the divorce was finalized outside of the first voluntary payment. While the divorce was in progress, I had vehemently requested that he have a paycheck deduction order for child support because I knew he wasn't going to pay on time, if at all. The attorneys negotiated for him to be allowed to pay voluntarily, and if he failed to do so, then I could seek an order for income deduction. Let's just say it took 10 years for that to happen and the state of Iowa to intervene. Parenthetically, the state of Iowa does not play when it comes to child support and custody. In the meantime, I had to find a way to support the two of us.

Over Christmas break in 1997, I interviewed for two other positions with Monsanto. One was with their Augusta, GA plant,

23

and the other was with their Luling, LA plant. Both interviews went well, and I received identical full-time offers from each plant. The offer included up to a 15% bonus based on individual, unit, plant, and company performance. The offer also included fully paid health, dental, and vision insurance as well as low-cost term life insurance and supplemental accidental death and dismemberment insurance with a 401k, including a guaranteed 3% match up to 6%, depending on company performance. As usual, they included a relocation package that would include furnishing allowances. This while I wasn't doing well in school at all.

I very distinctly remember being taken to lunch during my interview at the Luling, LA plant by six to eight other plant Black engineers. It already felt like home, as I had, for some reason, always felt connected to New Orleans. I can't say the same about Augusta, GA. So, there I was on New Year's Eve 1997 with three offers for full-time employment as a chemical process engineer with a Fortune 500 company as a salaried employee with benefits AND a PENSION (which had pretty much disappeared from corporate American benefits at the time)! All offers were contingent on me completing my bachelor's degree in chemical engineering. The HR representative from the Augusta, GA, plant called me to ask if I had made my decision. I really wasn't sure but then her next statement made it an easy decision. She said, "We're not going to get into a bidding war over you." At that point, I decided to take the Luling, LA offer at $46,000/yr with all the bells and whistle benefits ($90,148.54/yr in 2024 inflation-adjusted dollars). More details will be revealed in the social wealth section on how this changed my life.

In mid-January 1998, my parents bought me a used Chevy Cavalier to get back and forth to school, but it wasn't enough to resolve my financial issues. I continued to struggle with balancing classes and being a single mother. So, in the spring of 1998, I followed through on a tough choice and moved to Luling, LA. I started full-time as a chemical process engineer in May 1998, 32 credit hours short of my bachelor's degree in chemical engineering.

The Monsanto Years

My first working year as a full-time chemical process engineer was a whirlwind. I was assigned to a unit that was the bottleneck in the production of Monsanto's cash cow product Roundup® Weed Killer, so all eyes were on us to complete the production expansion project we'd been assigned. While I had significant financial debts hanging over me, I was so happy to be able to afford to pay for food and clothes again that I ignored the mountain of debts. I succumbed to "lifestyle creep," which I later learned in my MBA program is what happens when people make more money. It's psychological...**the more money you THINK you make, the more money you spend.**

"Lifestyle creep happens when increased income leads to increased discretionary spending. Lifestyle creep can take the form of an ever-escalating taste for the finer things or a growing slate of regular expenses that sap money from your savings account. Think higher and higher rent, hobbies that consume your cash, gourmet food, new and improved electronics, pets and kids, subscriptions and memberships, splurging on entertainment—you get the idea.

The problem with lifestyle creep is that it can edge out larger financial goals such as creating emergency savings, contributing to retirement funds, or putting money away for a down payment on a home. Without you realizing it, your newfound lifestyle can take priority over your financial security. Even if you are earning a generous income, you might end up living paycheck to paycheck or incur unaffordable amounts of debt. This kind of spending is heavy: If you experience any disruption in income or have an unexpected expense, you will almost certainly have trouble paying your bills." Gayle Sato, Money Matters Magazine.

This also reminds me of the book *H.E.N.R.Y. High Earner Not Rich Yet* by Gideon Drucker, CFP®, a book I later read that helped me get my finances on track. As a wealth coach, I carry this book in my purse with me everywhere I go.

First, it started with shopping for furniture. As part of my hiring package, executive relocation awarded me a stipend to furnish my new living space. I had never bought REAL furniture before, so I was excited! I was also terrified. What if I lost my job? Then, I would soothe those fears with the "baller" mentality, which, as described in the Urban Dictionary, means "Having the mindset *that no matter what happens in life, your* big baller ego lifestyle will supersede any financial or social strain on said lifestyle."

I went on shopping sprees in my free time, buying clothes and household items. I was happy to be what I thought of at the time as a REAL adult. I wanted to be like the upper-level engineers and managers, taking fancy vacations and investing in the latest IPOs (initial public offerings of stocks). I worked my behind off that first year and decided to treat myself to a nice vacation in the summer of 1999. I went to Maui, HI with a college friend who I had developed a crush on. While he and I were communicating, I shared my financial situation with him. He then shared a book with me that has since changed my life: *The 9 Steps to Financial Freedom: Practical and Spiritual Steps So You Can Stop Worrying* by Suze Orman.

At the time, I was researching car loans because the car my parents had given me had died. When I went out to get a car loan, my credit was trash because, during my first year of work I had ignored my student loans and medical debts, paying just the minimum on my credit cards even though I knew better. Just before the trip to Maui, I discovered that my car loan's interest rate was going to be in the double digits. I then thought about my financial situation and all the knowledge I had acquired about money up to that point.

It didn't make sense for me to have a double-digit car note interest rate. It didn't make sense for me to be paying interest on credit cards. It didn't make sense for me to be paying rent when I could afford a mortgage. I knew that because the Realtor® who put me into my townhouse rental reached out to me just before the trip and asked, "So, you ready to buy a house?" I thought back to my economics class, and I decided to make a change. I followed Suze Orman's 9 Steps as follows:

STEP 1: Seeing How Your Past Holds the Key to Your Financial Future

I thought back to how I was raised to be frugal and use education to earn money, invest and thereby become financially wealthy.

STEP 2: Facing Your Fears and Creating New Truths

Because I didn't have my BSChE degree, I was living in fear that I would lose my job. Having been on welfare, I never wanted to depend on anyone else for my income.

STEP 3: Being Honest With Yourself

I stopped ignoring my debts and took a comprehensive look at my financial situation. I started tracking my spending in money management software. I started spending less, paying down debts, and created a goal for myself to be a millionaire by the time I was 50.

STEP 4: Being Responsible to Those You Love

Over time, I followed her steps in this category and regularly updated my estate planning. Health wealth issues made this even more important as I got older and had a second child. I didn't want my children to be fighting over my estate the way I watched my mother fight with her sisters when my maternal grandmother died in 2001.

STEP 5: Being Respectful of Yourself and Your Money

From this I started taking advantage of the company 401k savings plan. In some years, I contributed up to the federal maximum amount. It wasn't until I later learned about Roth IRAs that I diversified my investments. The key takeaway here was that I learned to pay myself FIRST! I utilized dollar cost averaging as a strategy to invest in the retirement fund and maximize my returns. I also started the Harambee investment club with other employees at the plant so we could learn together and synergize our investment strategies.

STEP 6: Trusting Yourself More Than You Trust Others

I learned from Suze's book that I had more than enough knowledge to manage my own investments. To this day, major financial institutions court me for my funds so they can manage them. I find a low-cost index fund or exchange traded fund (ETF) is more favorable to most investors.

STEP 7: Being Open to Receive All That You Are Meant to Have

I started tithing and giving to charities but held off on loaning money to family and friends. I've always believed that loaning money can complicate relationships (social wealth), so I've never loaned more money than I could afford to give away. In one instance, when I was doing quite well, my parents asked to borrow money from me so they could pay down their credit card debt. I drew up a loan agreement, including interest charges, and had them sign it just to keep things clear. In my mind, if my parents never paid me back, I wouldn't have a problem with it, but I wanted to send a signal to the rest of my family about how I managed my money.

I still give to various charities both financially and with my time and knowledge wealth.

STEP 8: Understanding the Ebb and Flow of the Money Cycle

Through the investment club I started at Monsanto, I learned more about the stock market and started listening to Marketplace on NPR. I had always enjoyed economics, so I took a global view of financial markets and planned my own finances accordingly. Using the financial management software, I took a ten-year view of my personal finances and (which is key) planned accordingly.

STEP 9: Recognizing True Wealth

"One day, you'll be old, looking back at what seems important in retrospect. At that time, what in life would be of the most value? Probably not your net worth. So, don't measure your self-worth by your net worth. Decide what's really important in life and put it first." By Suze Orman

As I started implementing those steps, I instituted certain principles.

Pay yourself first.

29

As an employee it was a concept and principle I had never considered before. Pay myself FIRST?! I had never considered myself a financial priority. I had always been raised to pay my bills in full and on time, never to consider myself FIRST financially.

After reading that book, I made some significant financial changes in my life. I started saving in my 401k (unadvisedly at the time I maxed out my annual deposit). I put myself on a debt-elimination plan. Over the course of almost 11 years, I worked full-time for Monsanto, eliminated all of my consumer debt, improved my credit score, and accumulated significant retirement wealth. I was ahead of my time in creating a side hustle for myself in 2002 by becoming a certified aerobics instructor. I taught step, kickboxing, and yoga at a local gym for $12/class(hour) and didn't have to pay for a club membership. It was a small move but a start in the right direction financially.

When the Suze Orman show premiered on CNBC in 2002, I was glued to the television every Saturday night. I learned about budgeting, good debt and bad debt, and the power of compound interest (the rule of 72). I even managed to buy my first house in the summer of 2003, a 3-bedroom 2 bath 1745 square foot single family home for $141,000 ($241,033.37in 2024 inflation-adjusted dollars with a Zestimate of $260,700as of 09/05/2024). I put myself on a track that would set me up for financial freedom, but I wasn't done making financial mistakes like taking out a loan from my 401k to put a down payment on my first house or to help fund my current husband's business. One mistake I didn't make was holding on to the stock options Monsanto granted employees in 2001 and 2002 to prevent mass resignations when the company and economy were in trouble.

Over the years, as my income increased, I paid down debt, but I was repeatedly faced with the issue of lifestyle creep. I also considered my son's future when I had enough discretionary income to think about starting a college fund for him. It was Suze Orman's words from her show that changed my direction. **"Your child can take out a loan for college, but you can't take out a loan for retirement."** At the same time, I was watching my parents go through their preparation for retirement and I realized I couldn't depend on Monsanto's pension, and I needed to be prepared for higher healthcare costs. The chances of me still working for that company when I turned 65 were slim to none, and I needed to be prepared.

In 2006, I was offered a transfer from the Luling, LA plant to the Muscatine, IA plant. For knowledge and social wealth reasons, I sold my house in Luling for $185,000 ($288,640.38 in 2024 inflation-adjusted dollars) and bought a townhouse in Muscatine, IA, with the profits. Some people thought I was crazy buying a house at that time considering what was about to happen to the housing market. Thankfully, Muscatine, IA, was shielded from the housing crash, and I only lost $11,000 when I sold it in 2010 ($15,867.21 in 2024 inflation-adjusted dollars). It worked to our advantage by giving my current husband and I capital losses we could write off on our taxes.

It was during this season of my life that I also learned about tax preparation and Roth IRAs. In 2008, I had enough discretionary income to start saving in my Roth IRA. I started with $350/month, using as much of my discretionary income as I could to reach the $5000 2008 annual limit on contributions. In the following years, I built from there. I liked a Roth IRA better than a 529 plan or 401k because of the flexibility it offered. You see, 529 plan funds were required to only be used for education, and a 401k is taxed upon withdrawal and is only accessible without penalty after the account holder turns 59 ½ years old. With the Roth IRA, the funds grow tax-free, and the contributions are not taxed upon withdrawal (if the contributions are held for five years). In addition, Roth IRA fund deposits can be withdrawn for education, a first-time home purchase, or retirement.

I know I've mentioned Suze Orman's importance during this time of my life, so I must share this huge thing about it. I made it on to The Suze Orman Show as part of her "Can I Afford It?" segment in 2008. I asked her if I could afford to take my son on a trip to my father's homeland, Kenya, Africa. I laid out my finances for her producers prior to the show, and when I finally got to talk with her on camera, she was so impressed that I was APPROVED because my plan was to use my stock options to pay for the trip which at the time was going to cost about $10,000 ($14,609.18 in 2024 inflation-adjusted dollars). I ended up not taking the trip because shortly after that, my current husband asked me to marry him, and I used the funds to pay for our wedding.

When I started working full-time at Monsanto, I had a negative net worth of less than $40,000 in credit card, student loan, and medical debt ($77,187.73in 2024 inflation-adjusted dollars). When I left in 2009, I had accumulated $180,775.53 in 401k and Roth IRA retirement savings ($265,041.16 in 2024 inflation-adjusted dollars). After that, I had enough time to consider what I wanted to do with my life since I wasn't likely to get another job as a chemical engineer without a degree.

Because I had a passion for personal finance, I decided to become a financial advisor and got a job with Edward Jones in the spring of 2009. I worked for them off and on for about a year, including acquiring my Series 66 and Series 7 licenses. I later resigned due to significant health challenges. After that, I didn't work for over a year, but thankfully, I got married in October 2009, and my new husband was around to help support me and my son. Because we both had bad experiences in previous marriages, we agreed to sign a prenuptial agreement. At the time, my net worth as an individual broke down as follows:

ASSETS	VALUE
Taxable Investments	
Stocks, bonds, and funds	$-
Cash (savings and money-market accounts, CDs)	$18,257.79
Stock options (if exercisable)	$12,154.31
Real estate investments (not primary residence)	$-
Value of private business	$-
Value of other investments (Pension)	$30,745.98
Tax-advantaged investments	
Employer plans (401(k), 403(b), 457)	$141,492.22
Self-employment plans (Keogh, SEP)	$-
IRAs	$2,743.33
Education savings accounts, 529 plans	$-
Variable annuities	$-
Municipal bonds	$-
Personal property	
Primary Residence	$156,060.00
Vacation properties/second homes	$-
Art, collectibles, jewelry, and furnishings	$16,000.00
Other	11,545
Total Assets	**$388,998.63**
DEBTS	
Mortgages	$106,741.77
Home-equity loans	$-
Student loans	$-
Credit-card balances	$-
Other debt (Medical Bill for Surgery)	$2,300.00
Total Debt	$109,041.77
Term Life Insurance	$0.00
Supplemental Accidental Death Insurance	$0.00
NET WORTH	$279,956.86

I had also read the book *The Millionaire Next Door: The Surprising Secrets of America's Wealthy* and learned that net worth wasn't the best indicator of wealth, just like gross income is not the best indicator of wealth. I started tracking my "accumulator of wealth" score according to the instructions in the book, which were as follows:

	2008
Your household income (annual)	$82,281.01
Your age (average age for spouses)	34.0
Income times age	$2,797,554.49
Average net worth for someone of your age and income	$279,755.45
Assets minus inherited wealth	$389,798.63
Debt	$109,041.77
Net worth	$280,756.86
Final Score ----------------->	**1.00**

"Your wealth-building prowess is above average, but you'll have to improve to break into PAW territory." That was the assessment's rating for me.

PAW is short for a Prodigious Accumulator of Wealth. I wanted to be THAT kind of wealthy, and my new husband was on board with my vision.

Most of my wealth had come from investing in my 401k after I took care of some other critical financial housekeeping. First, I paid off my high-interest credit card debts. I had to choose between the avalanche method and the snowball method.

With the debt avalanche method, you'll focus on paying off your debt with the highest interest rate. This may mean you throw any extra cash you have at the debt while continuing to make minimum payments on your debts. Once you pay off that debt, you'll move on to the debt with the next-highest interest rate.

For example, let's say you have the following debts:

- A credit card with a 25% interest rate and a $1,000 balance
- A second credit card with a 15% interest rate and a $2,000 balance
- A gas card with a 22% interest rate and a $750 balance

Using the debt avalanche method, you would start paying off the credit card that has a 25% interest rate first, then the 22%, and finally the 15%.

However, paying off the highest-interest-rate debt first can take some time, so if you're eager to see results from committing to your financial plan, the debt snowball method might be a better option for you.

With the debt snowball method, you'll target your smallest debt first and use your extra money to pay off that one. The debt snowball method doesn't take your interest rates into account — instead, it's all about getting those quick wins to keep you motivated while repaying debt.

For example, if you owe your doctor $100, but your credit card has a $700 balance on it, and there are still thousands of dollars in student loans that you need to tackle, you'll pay off your medical bill first.

With both methods, how fast you pay off your debts and how much interest you save will depend on how much extra cash you must add to your monthly payment. I prefer the avalanche method, but there are calculators online that one can use to fit their personal relationship with money and motivation to pay off debt with the long-term goal of being debt-free.

Then, I started paying myself first by creating an emergency fund and maximizing my contributions to my 401k. I minimized spending and lived frugally, utilizing many cost-cutting skills I learned from my parents, but I still made time to enjoy traveling, especially to maintain relationships (social wealth). While at Monsanto, my 401k and other benefits were managed by Fidelity Investments. Little did I know I was being robbed through the mutual fund fees. Nonetheless, I managed to have accumulated $224,712.52 in retirement funds by the time my current husband and I started our next chapter, and that was going to come in handy.

The All County Years

In the spring of 2011, one of my husband's best friends and his wife asked my husband and I to join them for lunch. They were meeting with the owners of a real estate property management franchise they had bought into with territory in Orlando, FL. Because my husband's job at the Kennedy Space Center as a pyrotechnic engineer was ending when the space shuttle program ended in the summer of 2011, they wanted to know if we were interested in opening an All County real estate property management franchise with them in Brevard County (which is where the space center is). My husband had his own real estate company on the side and had his real estate broker's license since 2007, so it seemed like a reasonable fit for him. In their Orlando office, the husband had taken the lead after he took a severance package for his management position at Sprint. My husband was the broker for their office, while his best friend's wife had her real estate license and was studying for her real estate broker's license.

The three of them doing the deal seemed like a good transition for my husband, who had taken the lead as the financial provider

36

of our household since I had left my job as a financial advisor with Edward Jones in 2010 and was working on securing my bachelor's degree while managing my health. But things changed with my husband's best friend, and he and his wife had to pull out of the deal. So, my husband asked me to get my real estate sales associate license and help him run the franchise when the space shuttle program ended. I would still be able to go to school, but there was one catch. My husband would have to sink his entire retirement fund into the real estate property management business to capitalize on it. It was a HUGE risk!

By this time in my life, I had started weighing financial decisions in more than just financial ways. I was thinking from a holistic wealth perspective. For instance, would the others buying into the business be okay with us owning 35% and they own the rest. We'd be active in the business. And there it was. That little other word that had me scared...we! Over that summer, my husband got his exit package and put it in our joint account to live on while we got our financial lives together. Then, suddenly, his friend backed out of the deal to start the franchise office. I had literally just started taking classes at the local community college so I could complete my bachelor's degree in business administration. We were married, so I said, "What the heck!" and joined him in the business. We moved on to the song we'd listened to the year before when we were trying to figure out what we were going to do in our marriage...we did the "Unthinkable" (by Alicia Keyes).

We named the business Kizmet Inc., and my husband transferred his entire retirement account balance of $70,000 (or $97,883.43 in 2024 inflation-adjusted dollars) into the business account. Our property management business grossed $175 in 2011 (or $244.71 in 2024 inflation-adjusted dollars). Because we had no income and the housing market had tanked, we started praying about our situation.

We turned to church leadership at a marriage seminar and shared our situation with the group. When we asked what we should be tithing given that we had no income and what to do since we were upside down on an interest-only mortgage on our primary residence and the bank was refusing to work with us, the group leader asked us a few simple questions to give us direction:

"What does the Bible tell us we should tithe?"

To which we answered, "10% of your income."

"What is 10% of nothing?"

To which we replied, "Nothing!" and he said,

"Then that's what you should be tithing right now. Are you current on your mortgage payments?"

To which we said, "Of course!" and he then said,

"Then why would the bank work with you...stop paying the mortgage!"

So, we did. A year later, in 2012, we did a short sale on our primary residence while keeping my husband's first home as the rental property it already was. We moved from Orlando in Orange County, FL, to the neighboring east coast county of Brevard. We settled into a rental house in Rockledge, FL, just a ten-minute drive from our real estate property management office and right in the middle of our company territory.

I earned $0 from 2011 through 2014, while my husband collected some unemployment in 2011 and 2012. He then started earning income from the property management business in 2013. I felt some kind of way about him earning income from the business and me not taking anything home, so in 2014, I started getting some income from the property management business as well, with total income for the year equaling $12,000 (or $15,943.84 in 2024 inflation-adjusted dollars). The business was doing so well that we decided to move back to Orlando from Brevard County in the fall of 2014. We moved into my husband's rental property and started saving for a bigger home, given that our family was grow-ing. Literally two weeks after I graduated from The University of Florida with my Bachelor of Science degree in Business Adminis-tration, we conceived our first child together.

I received a nominal increase in pay from the business in 2015 for a total compensation of $25,750 (or $34,172.25 in 2024 inflation-adjusted dollars), and I was still feeling some kind of way about not receiving equal pay with my husband. So, in 2016, we started having our biweekly payroll match each other, and I received an annualized compensation totaling $70,000 (or $91,738.16 in 2024 inflation-adjusted dollars). In addition, be-cause my husband was itching for a new car, in the spring of 2016, we bought his almost dream car (at the time), a black 2014 Lexus GS 350. We also invested $35,000 (or $45,869.08 in 2024 infla-tion-adjusted dollars) into an All County real estate property man-agement franchise in the Jacksonville, FL area as partners with my husband's best friend and his wife. They'd already demonstrated success owning multiple All County offices in Florida and I had always wanted to open our original office in Jacksonville, so we thought it was a good idea. I spent a significant amount of sweat equity getting the office up and running that year.

In 2017, we changed our marketing strategy for the Brevard office and started including handling sales for owners we managed for but weren't referred to us for property management by a Realtor® doing sales for another business. Because the business had grown and we'd paid off all our consumer debt not tied to an appreciating asset (except for the Lexus), we decided we were ready to buy a bigger house in April 2017 and keep the Orlando house as an investment rental property. We bought a lovely five-bedroom, 3-bathroom, 3488 square foot waterfront home in Saint Cloud, FL (which is a suburb of Orlando to the south of the Lake Nona area with plans to make it our forever home) for $371,900

($477,225.14 in 2024 inflation-adjusted dollars). By the end of 2017, I had a slight increase in my annual income to $75,000 ($96,240.62 in 2024 inflation-adjusted dollars), which matched my husband's increase from the Brevard County business.

In the summer of 2018, I found myself ready to leave the real estate property management business for multiple reasons. I decided to go back to school to finally pursue the master's degree in business administration (MBA) I had been dreaming of since I was 7 years old. I thought the additional education would make me more valuable in the workplace when I graduated and went to work for someone else.

The following year, I significantly cut back on my hours in our Brevard County office as I focused more on my MBA. I immersed myself in the curriculum and let no worries about my student loans trouble me. In the fall of 2019, I started looking for employment in preparation for a spring 2020 MBA graduation. At the end of 2019, I again found that I didn't have an increase in my annual income of $75,000 (or $92,274.02 in 2024 inflation-adjusted dollars), so when New York Life asked me to interview for a financial advisor position, I thought it would be a great fit.

New York Life

In the spring of 2020, I was offered a full-time position with the Orlando New York Life sales office as a life insurance agent, contingent upon me obtaining my 2-15 Life, Health, and Variable Annuities license and digital proof of my MBA degree. In addition, if I met certain sales quotas in my first year, I would be first in line for a management position, given my MBA. Of course, things got interesting for the Brevard County office of our real estate property management company around that time because of the start of the pandemic. While I easily completed my 2-15 license in March of 2020, finishing my MBA while managing our Brevard County office through that crisis was an incredible challenge. We (like the rest of the world) had no clue what was going to happen to the economy with everyone having to quarantine.

I watched the news religiously. I kept thinking, if people can't go to work, how will they be paid? If they can't be paid, how will they pay their rent? If people don't pay their rent, what's going to happen to our business? We immediately evaluated all the possible outcomes and made quick decisions. We had to let someone go in our office so we let our administrative assistant go since that was work I could do from home. We stayed in close contact with our franchisor and followed their directions, which included applying for the Paycheck Protection Program (PPP) loans that the US government was administering to keep the economy afloat. We received $50,000 in PPP loan money ($60,766.35 in 2024 inflation-adjusted dollars).

Because New York Life wanted me in a captive contract based on commissions only, I delayed ending my income from our business until I had some income from New York Life. I ended the year 2020 with $35,878 in income ($43,603.50 in 2024 inflation-adjusted dollars).

Things got rocky again with the Brevard business in 2021. In May of that year, I had to step in and help my husband get a team together to support him. I wasn't really thrilled with my job with New York Life as I didn't find selling whole life insurance a good fit for my ministries, nor did I find selling term life insurance to be the best use of my time, and I couldn't seem to pass the series 7 exam again so I could start investing for my clients.

You see, I had prayed about my purpose in life and, through the assistance of some girlfriends, realized that my ministries were fourfold:

- Marriage
- Motherhood
- Money
- Mental Health

My husband and I strategically started our business called Hyphen Enterprises in the fall of 2021. We decided we'd focus our efforts on generational wealth and employ Robert Kiyosaki's ideas from *Rich Dad Poor Dad: What the Rich Teach Their Kids About Money That the Poor and Middle Class Do Not!pe* where he explains the four income quadrants. (The corresponding graphic is from the author's website.)

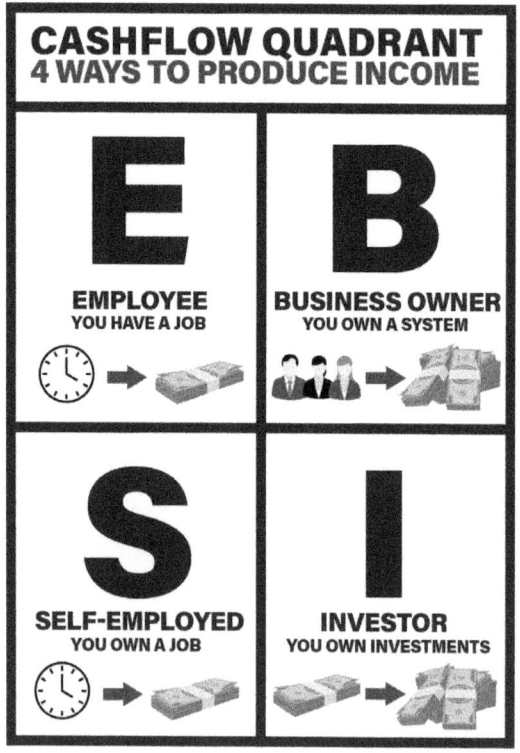

I kept thinking about retirement and how my husband and I were going to retire if we were always working in our own business. I thought about how much I enjoyed conveying financial literacy and my work with the award-winning non-profit organization 8 Cents In A Jar. I thought about integrity, accountability, communication, and teamwork...all the pillars of how we'd work to support our vision and mission. New York Life didn't align with all of that for me, and it showed in my sales commissions with the company. I ended the year with $10,818 of income ($12,557.46 in 2024 inflation-adjusted dollars). Other wealth factors (particularly health and financial) had me hold on to the job with New York Life through the end of the year, but at the end of the first month of 2022, I resigned from my position with New York Life.

I have watched my retirement portfolio grow over the years, and as of now, it's at an all-time high of $1,092,491.80 as of October 13, 2024. And that was just MY RETIREMENT. It didn't account for real estate, stocks, bonds, and businesses. I decided I had found my hedgehog after reading Socrate and Cassandra Exantus's book *Find Your Hedgehog and Stop Working: When You Find Your Passion, Work Stops Being Work.* As I eased into writing this book and building my new business, Lighthouse Wealth Coaching, I thought more about overcoming one of my greatest fears (spiritual wealth) and starting the path to public speaking.

The reality was I knew too much to be just anyone's employee anymore. I had spent years reading and listening to the financial industry powerhouses like Suze Orman, Dave Ramsey, and Marketplace on NPR. I had learned too much in my almost thirty years of being financially independent from my parents. I knew too much to think wealth was just about how much money you made in a year, or what you wore, or what car you drove, or what neighborhood you lived in. I had come to realize that wealth was built on so much more than money...and I was about to capitalize on that while I created generational wealth for my two sons. I'm now teaching both of my sons (who are 20 years apart) everything I possibly can to set them up for their futures.

Over the years, as my income increased (see my earning chart after this paragraph), I paid down debt, but I was repeatedly faced with the issue of lifestyle creep. I also considered my sons' futures when I had enough discretionary income to think about starting a college fund for them. It was Suze Orman's words from her show that guided my direction. **"Your child can take out a loan for college, but you can't take out a loan for retirement."**

The following are my Social Security and Medicare taxed work earnings to date according to the United States federal government website:

Work Year	Taxed Social Security Earnings	Taxed Medicare Earnings
1991	$1,227	$1,227
1992	$2,224	$2,224
1993	$6,309	$6,310
1994	$8,331	$8,331
1995	$1,448	$1,448
1996	$7,748	$7,748
1997	$10,016	$10,016
1998	$33,728	$33,728
1999	$51,640	$51,640
2000	$52,845	$52,845
2001	$56,015	$56,015
2002	$59,653	$59,653
2003	$60,641	$60,641
2004	$72,241	$72,241
2005	$76,446	$76,446
2006	$94,200	$102,759
2007	$85,387	$85,387
2008	$83,987	$83,987
2009	$57,170	$57,170
2010	$11,987	$11,987
2011	$0	$0
2012	$0	$0
2013	$0	$0
2014	$12,000	$12,000
2015	$25,750	$25,750
2016	$70,000	$70,000
2017	$75,000	$75,000
2018	$75,000	$75,000
2019	$75,000	$75,000
2020	$35,878	$35,878
2021	$10,818	$10,818
2022	$11,976	$11,976

Chapter 3

Part I

Knowledge Wealth:
Some Things You Learn Early

In a capitalistic society like America, we errantly often exclusively think of money or financial abundance as wealth. Through intentional subliminal marketing and other influences – including social media, we're socialized (for the most part) to be materialistic. However, since we're exploring the concept of multiple wealth currencies, we're going to shatter that errant concept.

When I was born in 1974, my mother said she looked into my eyes, saw the intelligence, and said, "You are going to be something FANTASTIC!" I hope I haven't disappointed her. While I was being born, my spirit was told by the other spirits (whom I believe to be my ancestors) told me to "look for the patterns." This is one reason I believe I've always been good at math. You see, from an early age, I knew that education, knowledge, and wisdom were important. Although I was physically little, I had three older sisters (five, seven, and 11 years older than me), and I felt big like them. Thus, I thought I should be doing what they were doing, and they were going to school every day. I eventually started asking my parents when I would be going to school and they would tell me, "When you get bigger."

At the time, I had three baby dolls. As a responsible mother, I didn't want them to worry when I went away to school. One snowy New Jersey morning, I put my coat and boots on and decided to walk to the nearby school and show my baby dolls (Matthew, Joey, and Elizabeth) where I would be going so they wouldn't get scared when their mother left them. The problem with this bright and mature idea was that this independent three-year-old DIDN'T inform her mother of her plans to leave the house.

My mother tells me she lost her mind when she realized I had left the house. She called the police, who helped her search our home to no avail. Thankfully, a neighbor several blocks away saw a little girl walking alone, didn't think it looked right, and called the police. My mother was greatly relieved when the police brought me home. She and my father promptly moved me from my babysitter's care to a daycare/early education pre-school part-time and told me it was school, so I would chill out. I was happy to be around my peers and learning.

I started my formal public school education in kindergarten in 1979. While zoned for Eastside High School (the school principal Joe Clark made famous in the movie *Lean On Me*), my older sisters were attending an experimental school called Dale Avenue. It was experimental in that the curriculum was quite different from the public school system we were zoned for, and my parents wanted their children to get the best education possible. One thing my father made very clear was he didn't want any unwed pregnancies from his daughters or substance abusers. Because both my parents were college graduates after growing up in poverty, education was of critical value for our family. The

48

same year I started kindergarten, a corporate headhunter sought out my father because of his newly granted patent for a hair care product. That company, Roux Cosmetics, was later acquired by Revlon Cosmetics.

My father decided to leave his job in New Jersey at Mennen Cosmetics and take a job in Jacksonville, FL, where the public schools were better. So, in the summer of 1980, my family moved from New Jersey to Florida. We moved to Mandarin, which was a predominantly White area of town, and it wasn't until we moved to Jacksonville that I even knew I was Black. The awakening to my existence as a Black child highlights a key part of what I attribute to knowledge wealth: knowledge of self. **Until we know ourselves, we cannot manage others' perceptions of us.** This is a critical part of emotional intelligence, which has been proven to be even more important than intellectual intelligence when it comes to success in Corporate America.

When the popular and groundbreaking *ROOTS* miniseries premiered on TV in the late '70s, my parents insisted that we watch it as a family. That series was my introduction to slavery and American history for Black people. Most of what I got from the movie was the importance of my African name, but the torment and defilement of racism had never been so personal until we moved to Florida. I was confused. My father also insisted that we watch the TV series *The Jeffersons* and *Good Times*. Through the shows, I knew *of* Black people with money and education and Black people struggling with money and education.

But how I learned I was Black is an ugly story, but here it goes. When we arrived in Jacksonville, our new house wasn't quite ready, so we had to stay at the Holiday Inn on Baymeadows Road, which at the time was "the White side of town." My father was at work the first day we were there, and my mother had five hungry kids (my cousin/newly adopted brother and my sisters and I) to feed, so she took us to the nearest Pizza Hut for lunch. We sat at a table. And sat. And sat. My mother tried to get service, and after an hour of waiting, a server finally told us, "We don't serve your kind here!" We left and went to a nearby McDonald's, but I was forever changed. Still, the racism didn't stop there.

When we finally moved into our home in the Pickwick Park neighborhood in Mandarin, we children were left alone while my parents went to work. While we were left alone at home, I still remember seeing the cross on our lawn from my oldest sister's bedroom window. The cross had the markings K-K-K on it. Later we'd learn that stood for Ku Klux Klan. I still remember hearing my oldest sister crying on the phone to our father. She told him that we wanted to go back to New Jersey. My father insisted we were staying! The police came and took a statement about the incident, but ultimately nothing was done.

One of the things we did every Saturday as a family was go to the downtown Jacksonville public library and check out books. Reading was one of my mother's favorite pastimes and my sisters and I had taken it on as a pastime as well. I used to dream of being a ballerina, a gymnast, or an ice skater, so I checked out the same two books every week: *A Very Young Gymnast* and *A Very Young Dancer*, both by author Jill Krementz. The ice skater dream died after we moved to Florida, but the ballerina dream was fueled by a dance school we always passed on the way to and from church. I would see the girls in their leotards and tights and dream of being a dancer like them. I nagged my parents enough that eventually, my mother stopped at the school one day when we saw other girls going in for class. We were promptly told that they don't take "our kind." Again, welcome to Florida, the Deep South, and racism. I didn't know it was going to show up in my education as well and significantly affect my knowledge wealth.

I started first grade in August 1980 in the Duval County public school system. My parents had to argue for me to be admitted to first grade because the birthday cutoff for kindergarten in Florida was in October, but in New Jersey, it was November. My parents argued that I had already sailed through kindergarten and there was no need for me to repeat it. They won, and I graduated high school at 17 years old because of their success.

Because of the ruling from *Brown vs. The Board of Education*, school busing had been implemented to desegregate the county's schools. Because early education is so critical in a child's development, the school system decided that children from the predominantly Black side of town (the northside) should be bused to the White side of town for their elementary education while middle school White children would be bused to the Black side of town for their middle school education. After that, children would go to high school in their respectively zoned neighborhood schools. Living in an all-White neighborhood, the only Black children I was exposed to in elementary school were of a lower socioeconomic background than mine. Because of that and my father's African heritage, I essentially didn't have the same cultural experience as the other Black children with whom I went to school.

I was regularly bullied by the Black children because of my lighter skin tone, African name, and how I spoke English. "You think you White!" one would exclaim. "You think you better than us!" another would shout. "You talk White!" I heard that one on numerous occasions. They didn't know that my father insisted we all speak proper King's English, the way he grew up knowing it in Kenya, which was subject to British colonization. It wasn't much better on the White side as they didn't know how

51

to take me. I ate lunch from the cafeteria with a food card like the kids on welfare. My mom made me go to the lunchroom and pay for the card every Monday morning with lunch money so my adopted brother/cousin and I wouldn't lose the money, and she wouldn't have to make our lunch. We looked poor, but we weren't. The rich kids' parents drove them to school, and they had cool lunch boxes with homemade lunches. I yearned for one of those lunch boxes and a healthy homemade lunch, never mind not having to take the school bus.

Even though I continued to live in the same house through my elementary, middle, and high school education, I changed schools quite often due to significant growth in Jacksonville and rezoning. In third grade, I was identified as a candidate for the gifted program. I was tested and scored just one point below the necessary 140 IQ to be admitted to the program. I remember my parents being called in about the results by a guidance counselor. He was a middle-aged White man, and he made it clear that while he thought I was bright, he didn't believe I (as he said), "a little Black girl," was gifted and didn't think I should be retested. My parents were disappointed.

My knowledge of who I was and how to fit in was even more evident when I realized I had no real friends in my neighborhood. Divorce was on the rise in the early '80s, and so broken families were plentiful, and dividing living arrangements were too. Often, kids were snatched out of their familiar homes to live elsewhere. There was one household with a rare new "blended family" in our neighborhood. The daughter played with me from time to time. Women were also exerting their independence in several ways including financially. Many were going back to work, and I distinctly remember the movie *9 to 5* with Dolly Parton, Lily Tomlin, and Jane Fonda which I often watched on HBO.

My neighbor's mom decided she wanted to go to work because her kids were both in school full-time. Her husband never wanted his wife to work, but my friend's mom decided to do so anyway. She hired a young woman as a babysitter to meet my friend and her younger brother at the bus stop at the end of the street each afternoon, walk them home, and stay with them until one of their parents came home. The babysitter was young and in her early 20s, had long brown hair and was thin. She was attractive, to say the least, and basically a younger version of my friend's mom. She drove a cute little Jeep and wore cute little outfits, and my mother noticed her right away. My friend's father drove a truck with the name of his pool company on the side.

One day, I was outside playing in the driveway when I noticed the babysitter's Jeep and my friend's father's truck both parked in the family driveway, but the kids and their mom weren't home. My mother noticed the kids and their mom coming up the street in their vehicle, and my mother quickly told me to go into the house and to my room. I went to my room, which was at the front of the house on the second floor and looked out the window. I heard yelling and screaming and fighting from their house. Shortly thereafter, my friend's mom walked out of the house to her vehicle with two suitcases and her two kids behind her. As they were getting in the car, both the father and the babysitter ran out of the house in towels. Apparently, they had been caught in an adulterous hookup. That was the last time I saw my friend.

Not long after that, the father married the babysitter, and they had a child together. In the ten years after that incident, the babysitter (who we learned was wife number three) never got a job, but she did have a baby to secure her future with the father, and as far as I know, she lived there until he died. The night of the incident, my mother said at the dinner table, "**Well, the way you** get them is the way you lose them." From that incident, I learned never to be the other woman.

In fourth grade, I was transferred to Beauclerc Elementary School due to rezoning again. By the spring of that school year, I was again identified as a potential gifted student by another guidance counselor. I was tested again. This time, I passed by focusing on what I remembered hearing as I was being born, "Look for the patterns." I started the gifted program in fifth grade at Beauclerc.

Around that same time, a typical Florida thunderstorm one night would introduce me to the world of insurance. A strange thing for a fifth grader to take note of, but one of those life things my parents would use as a teaching tool. During the storm, lightning hit one of the trees in our backyard and a branch broke off, fell, and put a small hole in the roof of our playroom. We didn't realize there was water damage from flooding in the room until a while later.

My parents filed a claim with their homeowner's insurance company for the flooding. Through their experience, I learned the difference between insurance damage due to falling water and rising water. The difference scientifically was obvious. Most homeowner's insurance policies don't cover rising water for damage. You need a separate flood insurance policy for that kind of damage. This information came in handy when, during college, my first husband and I had a flood in our duplex due to a toilet break. Thankfully, I had purchased renter's insurance, and we got a check for the damage to our property. That little bit of knowledge from my parents' experience turned out to be valuable. It has become even more obvious that there's a big difference between homeowner's and flood insurance with the remnants of Hurricanes Helene and Milton. Only 6% of homeowners have flood insurance, which is a grave mistake given climate change.

I share this and my youthful lesson about property values because it's important that the knowledge we learn and live as adults (parents, educators, etc.) be shared with kids of various ages. What they learn or inquire about may become resourceful wisdom. My parents remodeled their home twice during my school years. They would discuss how their over-improvement of the home would make it the most expensive house in the neighborhood. They said, "You don't want to be the most expensive house in the neighborhood. In fact, if you can, be the least expensive house in the neighborhood. That way, when another house in the neighborhood sells, it will bring up the value of your property." I kept that in mind for later real estate purchases. I also kept in mind when they said, **"Your house is only worth what someone else is willing to pay for it."** This was reinforced in college when I learned in economics class about supply and demand.

Interestingly, within months of that, insurance would become the class of the day again in our lives. I learned about life insurance when one of my father's friends, Mr. Ummana, died suddenly from a heart attack in his early 50s. He left behind his wife, Nneka and two sons, Obi and Choo Choo. They were from Nigeria, and generally, Africans don't believe in life insurance. I babysat her sons for some extra money during spring break over a couple of years. It wasn't a pleasant experience for me; the challenges for them and us during that time stayed in my mind. They also motivated me to be sure I had life insurance once I had children.

While I was gaining so much real-world knowledge at home in our family life, I was also seeing how things around you that you see can suddenly be illuminated in your knowledge wealth. For example, in fifth grade at Beauclerc, I was in a team-teaching class and during my gifted session, we dissected a cow's stomach together. We could see actual grass inside the full stomach. I still remember thinking, "Well, that makes sense when you see cows grazing on grass all day." It also planted the seed for me to later realize I didn't want to go into anything in the medical field.

In sixth grade, I was bused across town to RV Daniels Sixth Grade Center (in a not-so-great part of town). In seventh grade, I was zoned for Matthew Gilbert Seventh Grade Center (in another not-so-great part of town) but instead enrolled at Stanton College Preparatory School. At the time, it was a cutting-edge seventh through twelfth-grade college preparatory school designed to educate Duval County's best and brightest as the county's second magnet school. I did fine there in seventh grade. My mother was over the moon one afternoon talking to my father about my pre-algebra class and how I understood "the empty set" of Venn diagrams. But my grades got progressively worse in eighth grade.

They got so bad that I was kicked out of Stanton at the end of eighth grade because I got a D in U.S. History and an F in English. Even though I was great at math, I only squeaked by with a C in Algebra. I was boy crazy and depressed. I was in relationships with 16-year-old boys when I was 12. I was skipping pre-algebra at the end of the day to make out with a little White boy.

My parents were distraught. They thought the only solution was to enroll me in private school over the summer to help me catch up. At that time, Duval County school rules required that any child who didn't pass English be held back a year. Even though I was on track to graduate at 17, my parents didn't want me in high school any longer than necessary. They had my third sister take me to The Bartram School, which was a private school. As I sat in the headmistress's office thumbing through the yearbooks while they finished my enrollment, I noticed that there were only pictures of girls. Then it hit me...it was Bartram School for GIRLS! I went for the summer of 1988, where I was tutored daily in U.S. History and Algebra. I received credit for the Algebra class so I could proceed to the next level in math. For where we lived, I was zoned to go to Alfred I duPont Junior High for eighth and ninth grade.

When I finished my summer at Bartram, I enrolled in duPont for ninth grade, my first grade of high school. I had started learning about basketball since Michael Jordan had caught my attention. I joined the girls' basketball team to fit in. My parents arranged for me to do both a whole year of eighth and ninth grade English simultaneously and for all my classes to be honors classes. This included honors geometry. I did fine throughout the year in that class but didn't earn straight As. When I took the final exam, I found it quite easy and passed with 100%. The teacher (an older White male) didn't believe I could have possibly earned that grade without cheating, so he called my parents in for a conference. My parents explained to him that I had always been gifted with math, and this was no surprise to them. The teacher insisted I cheated so he made me take the exam again in the classroom alone. When I aced that exam, he was shocked. He said that had never happened before with a little Black girl.

At any rate, after ninth grade, I was zoned for tenth through twelfth grade at Wolfson Senior High School. Between ninth and tenth grade, I applied to return to Stanton because there, my intelligence had never been questioned, but I was denied re-admission. I wasn't happy about having to attend Wolfson, but I made the best of it by taking as many honors classes as I could. At the end of the year, I applied for a return to Stanton again. I was denied again. Mandarin was growing so quickly that the county had to build yet another high school, and I was rezoned yet again. This time, I was supposed to attend Mandarin High School for 11th and 12th grade. They offered advanced placement (AP) and dual enrollment classes, so I figured I could make the best of it and dug in. Then, my world changed.

Over Labor Day weekend in 1990, a call came to our home phone. It was a guidance counselor at Stanton calling to say that they had reconsidered my application for readmission and changed their minds. I was to start class at Stanton the next day! It wasn't until many years later that I learned my mother had seen how devastated I was not being at Stanton and had "made some phone calls" to get me back in (social wealth).

I went back to Stanton College Preparatory School in September 1990. I was enrolled in a Humanities dual enrollment class as well as AP English I, AP American History, Honors Physics, Honors Pre-Calculus, and various other classes. I did well, including passing both of my AP exams with 3s. On AP exams scores ranged from 1-5. Scoring 3 and higher earned you college credit. My father suggested I take preparation classes for my SAT. I had long ago learned one of the most valuable knowledge wealth lessons: **"It's much cheaper to learn from other people's mistakes than to have to learn by making the mistake yourself."**

My parents had previously paid for my second and third older sisters to take SAT prep classes, hoping they would do well enough on the exams to qualify for college scholarships. One night, when they were both supposed to be in the prep class, they got into a car accident, taking another student home instead of attending class. My parents found out from the police report that they weren't where they were supposed to be, and neither of my sisters did well enough on the standardized tests to get scholarships.

One went away to the University of Florida for three semesters, and at the same time, the other unmarried sister finished her senior year of high school and enrolled in the local university; both ended up living at home under my parents' control. Each of my sisters essentially went from our father's house to a home with a husband. I took a different path. I also took the SAT preparation class after I scored 1170 on the exam the first time cold. After I took the prep class and took the SAT exam again, I scored 1300, which included a damn near perfect score on the math portion. Okay, maybe 730 is not as close to the perfect 800 you would describe, but it was good enough for me since my math score jumped over 100 points. Especially good enough to translate my knowledge currency of high standardized test scores and weighted grade point averages into financial wealth through scholarship money for college. I also did well on the PSAT exam. Well, enough to be named a National Merit Scholarship Finalist and National Achievement Scholar. That had the college scholarships pouring in, which was yet another example of the currency exchange between financial and knowledge wealth. I had used my knowledge wealth to gain financial wealth through scholarships, grants, and paid internships.

Chapter 3

Part II

Knowledge Wealth: As You Grow, You Know

This FAMU Rattler, as you have read by now, attended her alma mater having been awarded the Life Gets Better Scholarship. I chose chemical engineering as my major from a financial and knowledge wealth perspective, and it seemed like a good fit. But honestly, I still had to learn what I have coined in my maturity as the **7 Things Every College Student Should Know About Money**:

1. The difference between grants and loans (OPM – Other People's Money) What the interest rates are for all loans and credit cards (Rule of 72)
2. How compound interest can work both for and against you (Rule of 72)
3. Credit cards are tools, not toys
     a. Points are there to get you to spend more money (Customer Lifetime Value or, as I learned it in my MBA program, CLTV).

4. A luxury once enjoyed becomes a necessity (again, lifestyle creep).
5. Saving and investing now and for the future (Rule of 72)
6. Investing is easy and start NOW! (Rule of 72)
7. How to function on a spending plan (or budget, which is not a bad word) and avoid consumer debt (It's not about buying power, it's about paying power).

You see the **Rule of 72** there repeatedly, but I didn't really learn its power and the power of compound interest for another decade. The rule estimates the amount of time required to double any amount invested with a fixed interest rate. It's one of many financial rules in the finance industry.

Shortly after high school graduation, I was driving the former family station wagon to the Jacksonville airport to catch a flight to the New York City area. I was listening to the radio when "Under The Bridge" by Red Hot Chili Peppers came on. I couldn't help but think of the recent headlines in newspapers and reports on television and radio news. One of the most terrifying world events then was the riots in Los Angeles because of the Rodney King incident. Those riots made me wonder how things were in my old neighborhood in NJ since racism in America hadn't seemed to improve as a result of the previous LA Watts riots.

I was looking forward to seeing my Uncle Smiley (who was really my dad's cousin, Francis K. Gichia), who was always at our house in Paterson. I was also looking forward to going up to Nyack, NY, to visit my Aunt Edna and Uncle Neal (short for Cornelius) Underwood. My Uncle Neal was my maternal grandfather's brother, and they were my second sister's godparents. Since I didn't have godparents, they were surrogate godparents for me. Ultimately, though, I was looking forward to seeing my great-aunt, Leona Washington (my maternal grandmother's sister), and my great-grandmother, Bertha Brown (my maternal grandmother's mother), most. In the family, we called my great-grandmother Goggie because, as children, we could not say "Great Grandma." Goggie was born in North Carolina in 1902, so she was almost 90 years old when I went to visit her that June. I had grown up with the value of respecting your elders, and the wisdom they held was considered invaluable. That week with my family elders was my high school graduation gift to myself, and I paid for it with the newly created frequent flier miles on Delta Airlines from our last trip to Kenya.

While I was in New Jersey, my Uncle Smiley took me to visit our old house. It looked much smaller as a 17-year-old adult than it did as the small five-year-old girl who had left there 12 years earlier. When I spent a day or two with my Aunt Edna and Uncle Neal, I witnessed firsthand what dementia looked like. My uncle sat at the breakfast table weeping like a four-year-old boy over his cereal, stuck in his tortured memory. Lastly, I enjoyed several days in Lindenhurst, Long Island, NY, with Goggie and her daughter, my Great Aunt Leona. All week long, Goggie kept asking me if I wanted to be around people my own age since she was almost 90. I kept telling her, "No, Goggie. I want to spend time with you!"

Finally, that Friday, she and my Great Aunt Leona took me shopping. I had a thing for hats back then, so Goggie (who liked hats too) bought me a nice black hat. On the way home, she said to me, "Tonight, you're going bowling with some of the kids from my church."

To which I replied, "Okay."

When we got back to her house, she said to me, "Now, when you get back tonight, if you see my door is closed, don't knock. Now let me show you my new bed!"

I looked at her, surprised at her excitement, but said, "Okay," as I followed her into her room.

She showed me her Craftmatic adjustable bed with pride and exclaimed, "The government bought this for me because I'm on social security." She was so happy to have social security! She didn't think the US government would see her live as long as she did, and truthfully, when social security was created, it was only intended for people to live up to five years after receiving it, not the 20 or so years people live now.

That night, I went bowling with the kids from her church. When I got back, her door was closed, so I didn't knock and went to bed. When I woke up in the morning, I walked into the kitchen to find my Great Aunt Leona sitting at the kitchen table in her nightgown and slippers with a glass of brandy. I looked over at the kitchen stove, and there was an old Black man cooking in his undershirt and boxers, with his socks pulled up to his knees.

He turned around to me and said, "Oh, you must be Bertha's great-granddaughter! How do you like your eggs?"

I was a bit surprised and taken aback but responded, "Scrambled?"

Great Aunt Leona then motioned for me to come over and sit next to her at the table, which I did. She then leaned over close to me and whispered, "I got me a young one. He is in his 70s!"

And that's all I have to say about that. Well, not quite. During that trip, I learned that my Great Aunt Leona was actually older than my grandmother, but she looked, seemed, and behaved so much younger. I asked her how she stayed looking so young, and she shared three things that have been burned into my memory ever since:

1. A little bit of alcohol every day.
2. A little bit of Oil of Olay every day.
3. Find out what the kids are doing.

I was always inspired by my great-grandmother and great-aunt's wisdom. I feel blessed to have known them and spent that time getting to know them. I've made it a personal goal to try to live to be 102 (My Creator willing), two years longer than Goggie, just for the heck of it.

After I returned home from up north, I worked the summer of 1992 at the Monsanto Chemical plant in Pensacola, FL. I learned a lot about safety protocols in the workplace, carpet and tire yarn manufacturing, and manufacturing in general. I learned so much as an intern that was invaluable in the workplace, though I didn't realize it then.

I started studying at FAMU knowing how important it was to keep my grade point average up to keep my scholarship, so I figured it made sense to ensure A grades in as many classes as possible and beef up my grade point average before I got to the more difficult upper-level chemical engineering classes. African-American History and Introduction to Engineering rounded out my first-semester class schedule. I learned so much in those two classes.

African-American history built on what I had learned about Black history in my AP American History class. I found pride in my people and what they had done. I had a better understanding of the need for HBCUs. Another significant class for me during the first semester of my freshman year was Introduction to Engineering. Three graduate students taught the class: Paul Philpott (a White guy with a biracial daughter), Michael Robertson, and Jesse Ingram. They taught us how Corporate America worked and how to research companies that manufactured products we used so we could invest in them. Most importantly, they taught us how credit cards worked, the importance of paying more than the minimum on credit cards, and that credit card debt was a modern-day form of slavery/indentured servitude. Hats off to those graduate students. It's part of why I am retired at 49!

I also encountered my first corporate networking event as a first-semester freshman. FAMU used to have what they called Cluster every spring and fall semester. They'd bring in corporate representatives from all the companies that were sponsoring scholarship students and offering scholarships. My Monsanto corporate representative would come down each semester. The first semester I was unsure of whether to attend the networking event at all. I was told by my scholarship coordinator that it wasn't required but was *strongly suggested*. I was told to wear my best suit to look the corporate part. I didn't have a suit, and I was reluctant to spend any money since I was living on a limited stipend and didn't want to run up a credit card bill. My scholarship coordinator said to me, "**You've got to spend money to make money.**"

I bought an appropriate suit that afternoon and wowed many of the corporate representatives when I attended that Cluster. I shared the experience with my parents and the fact that I had bought my first suit with my own money before I was 18. Their response was to ask me to come home for my birthday so they could take me to Dillard's department store, where my dad was working and buy me the most expensive suit they could find. They also insisted on buying a pair of earrings and a necklace. I tried to accept their gifts with grace as I needed a suit for Cluster weeks before my birthday.

You see, I started college shortly after my father had taken an early retirement package from Revlon. There was a dispute about his date of birth, and in the process of settling it, we discovered that we'd been celebrating the wrong birthday for him. We always celebrated August of 1937 instead of his actual birthday in September of 1935. They ended up paying him more than they anticipated (one month for every year of service with the company) because of the discovery of his original birth certificate.

My second semester of freshman year got really interesting. I was enrolled in 19 credit hours, including Fortran computer coding. I ended up withdrawing from the Fortran class because **I learned that soaking up knowledge has its limits, just like a sponge soaking up water.** I simply didn't have the capacity to make straight As in those 19 credit hours of classes while working at night for the SAFE team. At the same time, I ended the semester with a 4.0 grade point average and on the dean's list, so from a strategic perspective it was a good move.

When I graduated from high school, started college, and prepared to go to work with a Fortune 500 company, I did so with a wealth of knowledge about how to be a good employee:

- If you're early, you're on time. If you're on time, you're late.
- Give it your best shot.
- If you don't know, ask somebody.
- Be willing to work overtime for the good of the team.

I started my internship in the summer of 1993 with Monsanto company in Pensacola, with no specific learning goal in mind but that knowledge. My knowledge wealth at that point had increased significantly thanks to the Life Gets Better Scholarship program training sessions. Those training sessions taught me how to play "the game" that is Corporate America. Some examples include managing others' perceptions of you and the differences between a manager, a supervisor, a mentor, and a sponsor. In the fall of 1993, I started taking upper-level chemical engineering classes. The one that stands out in my mind is the Introduction to Chemical

Engineering class and the simple formula the class was based on: In – Out = Accumulation + Generation. They were teaching it to apply to chemical processes, and I didn't do well in the class. I earned a D. I couldn't quite make the transition to the abstract thought required to apply the concept to chemical processes. In retrospect, my internships up to that point gave me more research than manufacturing process exposure, so the application to chemical processes was difficult for me. I did have to retake the class in the spring of 1994. I did learn how to apply the formula to chemical processes. Still, I also realized it applied to money as well, which crystallized things for me. I ended up completing the class with a B.

That academic year, I enrolled in more upper-level chemistry courses (as requisites for the chemical engineering degree), including Organic Chemistry I with lab. In that class, I learned that Carbon is the key to organic chemistry. I also took Physics with Calculus and Lab, Elementary French (for the grade point average boost), Statistics, and Introduction to Sociology. After the sociology class I called my parents and told them I was thinking of changing my major to social work. I previously called them and told them I was considering changing my major to FAMU's five-year MBA program after seeing the FAMU School of Business and Industry students walking across campus in their suits going to forum each week. While this wasn't the first time I had called home and told my parents I was considering changing my major from chemical engineering, their response wasn't different. They lost it and reemphasized to me that people with those degrees don't make as much money as chemical engineers. In addition, I would have to give up my scholarship and internships to pursue those majors, likely having to take out student loans to pay for my education. I ended up not changing my major because of what I had learned: **It's much cheaper to learn from other people's experiences than to have to go through it yourself to learn the lesson.**

I decided to focus and did well in my fluid dynamics (Transport Phenomena I) class that year. I ended up retaking and completing my Fortran class in the Spring of 1994 and squeaked out a C. That summer, my knowledge wealth expanded in ways affected by my social and health wealth, least to say my financial wealth. I returned to FAMU in August 1994 without a car, unmarried, and pregnant at 19 years old. I had to learn very quickly how to manage during a crisis and to do so as independently as possible.

I started the next academic year of chemical engineering classes in the Fall of 1994 by enrolling in the next set of classes. This included Transport Phenomena II (heat transfer, which I loved), chemical engineering thermodynamics, and engineering mechanics. In addition, I took public speaking and Statistics I. It was a heavy load, and a couple of my engineering class grades suffered, but I made it through the semester with my scholarship intact, even though I was pregnant with my first child.

On December 20, 1994, I learned what it felt like to say, "I do," when I married my baby's father. I only had a few months to practice being a wife before I had to add learning how to be a mother. I was so focused on studying for my Spring 1995 classes that I did fairly well in most of them. One class that I failed (Organic Chemistry II Lab) was a class where the professor asked me why I was even bothering to come to class since I was pregnant. Ironically, I started labor during that course's final exam, and just over twenty-four hours later, I knew what giving birth was like. Still, I had yet to learn what it meant to be a mother. I spent a couple of weeks trying to be a stay-at-home mom at the suggestion of the Monsanto HR representative. I struggled. We needed income, so after six weeks of maternity leave, I pulled the classifieds out of the newspaper and started looking for a job. I found work as a temporary employee with the state of Florida. I developed some of my computer skills over that summer.

I enrolled in school full-time in the fall of 1995 for what was my fourth year as a chemical engineering major at FAMU. I continued with courses like Transport Phenomena III (Mass Transfer), Physical Chemistry I with Lab, and Environmental Engineering, and repeated courses like Introduction to Electrical Engineering with Lab. I struggled to balance classes with marriage and motherhood. My husband and I arranged our class schedules so one of us was always with the baby since we could not afford daycare. This arrangement wasn't favorable to my nor my husband's grade point averages. My husband's grades were so low he no longer qualified for financial aid. If he was going to school, it was going to be on student loans and because his credit was so bad, that meant I was going to be financially responsible for those loans as well.

In the Spring of 1996, my parents stepped in to offer financial help. They offered to pay for daycare for the baby so both of us could go to classes unhindered during the day. This would allow my husband to continue to work at night. We took the assistance. My grades were good enough for me to hold on to the scholarship for another year and to secure another internship with Monsanto for chemical engineering that summer. I requested a different location this time as I knew there were multiple chemical sites within the company worldwide. I was grateful that I knew the headquarters for the company was in Saint Louis, MO, so when an offer came to do my summer internship at a plant just outside the city, I jumped at it.

In the summer of 1996, I worked as a chemical engineering intern at a food additives plant. During my previous internships with Monsanto, I learned a lot about safety and the Occupational Safety and Health Administration (OSHA), but at this plant, I learned even more about both as well as the Food and Drug Administration (FDA) because the plant manufactured phosphorus-based food additives. I also improved my computer skills as I spent the entire summer redrawing plant engineering flow diagrams (EFDs) in the software program Visio. It was really an administrative job, but it gave me a place to start applying the abstract chemical process knowledge I had been getting from my college courses.

As I mentioned in the financial wealth section, I came home from work one August day to discover my then husband had left with our son. I had no idea where my child was, whether he was safe, or if I would ever see him again. I learned how broken our legal system is and how it works so much better for your benefit if you have money. My crisis management skills went into overdrive as I had to demonstrate knowledge of all five wealth currencies just to survive.

I went back to FAMU in the middle of August 1996 and enrolled in my next academically advised set of classes. At this point I was at least a semester behind many of my freshman year chemical engineering counterparts as far as progress towards my bachelor's degree. I was distracted by personal problems, and once I got physical custody of my son back midsemester, I was thrown into single motherhood. I didn't do well academically and wasn't sure what else to do but keep trying to finish the degree. The next Spring, I enrolled in yet my next academically advised set of classes, and I continued to learn about balancing life as a single mother while going through a bitter divorce.

When I was offered yet another chemical engineering internship with Monsanto for the summer of 1997, I again saw an opportunity and jumped at the chance. I continued interning with Monsanto at their Muscatine plant for that summer. I learned a lot about manufacturing the intermediate ingredients for one of their leading weed killers. I also spent my free time building a Microsoft Access database (including coding in SQL) for my music collection (also known as "The Trunk of Funk"). I had been told that I didn't need a degree to work as a database manager if I knew how to write database code. I would put my son to bed at night and work on the database on my PC at home. More importantly, I had the time and space I needed to start putting together a plan. Granted, I wouldn't complete the plan for another two years, but I at least became painfully aware that I needed one if I was going to become wealthy.

In the summer of 1997, I came across a poster titled "How To Be A Succulent Wild Woman" by Sark. The poster was a list which read:

- "Bathe naked by moonlight.
- Marry yourself first. Promise never to leave you.
- Buy yourself gorgeous flowers.
- Practice extravagant lounging.
- Invent your life over if it doesn't feel juicy.
- Cradle your wounded places like precious babies.
- Be delicious.
- Eat mangoes naked. Lick the juice off your arms.
- Discover your own goodness.
- Smile when you feel like it.
- Shout: I am here! I am succulent and I am loud!
- Be rare, eccentric, and original.

- Describe yourself as marvelous.
- Paint your soul.
- Investigate your dark places with a flashlight.
- Make more mistakes!
- Weave your life into a net of love.
- Tell the truth faster.
- Celebrate your gorgeous friendships with women.
- You are enough. You have enough. You do enough."

Those words changed me. I bought the poster and kept it with me when I moved back to FAMU. I drove by myself across the country from Muscatine, IA, in a U-Haul with my two-year-old son. We spent one night in Tennessee with a woman I had met in a divorce website chat room. After that, you couldn't tell me I didn't know how to manage a crisis independently, even though I was only 22 years old.

Once again, I jumped into advised classes...sort of. I started taking all the classes a senior in chemical engineering would take, whether I was prepared for them or not. I was delusional. I thought, *"If I can just take all of these classes, somehow I will magically pass them all, graduate, and be able to get a decent job!"* I was no longer delusional when I had to take out the first set of student loans to pay for all those classes since my grades had dropped so low I was no longer eligible for the Life Gets Better or any other scholarship.

In the spring of 1998, I continued my strategy of taking senior-level classes since it hadn't gone all bad the previous semester. I remember waking up at 5:30 in the morning to get myself and my son ready, so I could walk from my apartment at least half a mile (listening to "In Due Time" by Outkast) with my purse, backpack, baby's diaper bag, and stroller to the nearest bus stop. Along the way, I would sing the lyrics of the bridge of the song, which emboldened me.

When we'd get to the bus stop, I would take the first bus to the transfer station downtown and take yet another bus to the not-so-great part of town where I could afford daycare. I would drop Shorty (my first-born son's nickname, which was common for children and girlfriends in the mid-90s) off and then literally run uphill from the daycare to the FAMU campus, where I would catch the only bus to the FAMU/FSU Engineering building that got there by 7:00 am which is when the Introduction to Electrical Engineering class was scheduled. It was required (along with the lab) for every Chem E student. I struggled with that class. I had done quite well in my mass transfer lab since it was group work, and I was assigned to work with a group of males (two White from FSU and one Black from FAMU).

I started working full-time as a chemical process engineer at the Monsanto Company in Luling, LA plant in 1998. On my first day, I met with the human resources (HR) representative who was managing the influx of plant new hires (the plant was growing significantly). I was assigned to the DSIDA unit, which manufactured disodium iminodiacetate, which is a precursor in the manufacture of glyphosate, the active ingredient in Roundup® herbicide. The HR rep was ready to walk me over to the unit but wanted a copy of my transcript in a sealed envelope. I panicked! I told her that my transcript was locked in my file cabinet, which had been in transport with my things on the moving truck. She understood how the relocation process could be overwhelming and stressful and told me to get it to her within the week.

I went home that night and thought long and hard about what I was going to do. I pulled my transcript in the sealed envelope out of my file cabinet and looked at it. I considered opening the envelope. I knew my grades wouldn't be different if I opened the envelope. I decided to take my chances and took the sealed envelope with me to work the next day. I thought of the succulent wild woman poster words: "Tell the truth faster" as I dropped the envelope off in the HR representative's mailbox. I then went on to the unit. I had a lot to learn as I was new to the plant, the process, the city, the state...EVERYTHING! And I was terrified because **I didn't know what I didn't know.** What I did learn was how to function with a secret and that **"Secrets and lies are two ends of the same rope that keep us in bondage"** (spiritual wealth).

Over the next couple of weeks, I met with various people in the plant, including the unit supervisor, the unit technician supervisor, the unit maintenance supervisor, chemical process engineers in each of the key process units, and the Black female unit business unit leader who'd hired me. I was inundated with information about how the plant worked, how the process worked, how the business worked, etc. Engineers of all kinds came to my office, including chemical process, maintenance, mechanical, electrical, instrumentation, production, and environmental engineers. They were leaving manuals, manufacturing process books, books of engineering flow diagrams, books of process flow diagrams, and more! I had safety training, environmental training, and process training, and that wasn't all! I was immersed in Corporate America, and I had limited game.

While I had always had an above-average intelligence quotient (IQ), my emotional intelligence (EQ) wasn't as well developed. My social skills were lacking as I'm a natural introvert and had limited social interaction outside my family while growing up. College is often an opportunity for young adults to develop their social skills and emotional intelligence through interactions with their peers. My college experience was limited socially because

I chose such a challenging major and became a mother and wife so young. Those responsibilities forced me to prioritize financial wealth for the survival of myself and my son for most of those years. However, now that I was out of college and living just outside of a party city like New Orleans, being newly single, I saw an opportunity to improve my social skills (wink wink).

One thing that became abundantly obvious extremely quick to many of my coworkers was that I needed to increase my EQ if I was going to be successful. I personally wasn't aware of this and spent my first year as a chemical process engineer working in one of the biggest global supply chain bottlenecks to produce the most in-demand herbicide on the market at that time, and it was like being thrown in the ocean in a rip tide without fully knowing how to swim. I nearly drowned professionally. I was so happy to be out of survival mode financially that I neglected many areas of wealth in my life, including finances. I knew I had to do something and do it right.

So, in the summer of 1999, I started learning about personal finance after reading personal finance guru Suze Orman's book *The 9 Steps to Financial Freedom: Practical and Spiritual Steps So You Can Stop Worrying*. I also read Thomas Stanley's book *The Millionaire Next Door* and started calculating my net worth and accumulator of wealth score. I started cleaning up my credit and taking care of old collections debts. I started learning how credit scores were calculated and how to improve mine. I started learning more about investing and started investing in my company's 401k. I started tracking my income and expenses in personal finance software like Microsoft Money and Quicken. I also put myself on a spending plan. I put together a plan to pay off my car loan in three years, as well as a plan to pay off my student loans, credit card, and medical collections debts. I even helped lead the

Harambee (which is Swahili for "Let's Pull Together") investment club with other minorities at the plant. That was great and perfect timing because, around the same time, I was put on a performance plan at work.

My new boss explained to me that the performance plan meant that I had one month to perfectly demonstrate the specific knowledge, skills, and abilities required of my job, or I was no longer going to be employed with Monsanto. Under my new supervisor's guidance, I started working on my emotional intelligence. My boss's supervisor (the Black female who'd initially hired me) made some changes to management in the DSIDA unit, which included instituting an engineering supervisor, thus leaving the unit supervisor as the manager of our unit while he reported to her. He took a particular interest in me being successful because it was going to show how successful he was as a leader. I was a test of his leadership and EQ.

I managed to make it through the performance plan and hold on to my job. One of the more experienced Black lab technicians (with whom I had built a rapport) then pulled me aside and said, "Play the game!" I had heard that if you want to succeed in Corporate America, you should learn how to play chess (think organizational charts). I had never learned how to play chess, and it showed. He pointed out to me that I wore t-shirts and jeans to work instead of collared shirts with khakis (which is what management wore). Seemingly small things to me, like what I wore or not wanting to take on tasks I didn't feel were mine, said so much about me that my new boss nearly fired me for insubordination.

My new boss (an older Black male engineer) came to me one day and asked me to upgrade an Excel spreadsheet that he was using. I had exceptional computer skills, but being a bit older, the Office Suite software was a bit of a challenge for him to master. I listened to what he wanted me to do and determined it was an administrative assistant type assignment and told him, "No, I'm not doing that." You read that right. I directly told my boss, "No," to an assignment he was giving me. He looked incredibly angry and reiterated that he was my boss, and I was supposed to do what he told me to do. I then responded that I was an engineer and wasn't going to be relegated to doing administrative work. He told me he was going to put a letter in my file and walked out of my office. I thought for a minute after he left about what I had done and shortly thereafter went to my coworker.

When I shared what I had done with my coworker across the hall, who was a slightly older, well-liked, White female senior engineer, she quickly told me what to do to save myself. I did exactly as she told me, went to my boss, and apologized. I also asked her to mentor me when I realized **my EQ/EI** (based on the 1995 bestselling book *Emotional Intelligence* by science journalist Daniel Goleman) **was going to affect my net worth and, thus, my net wealth**. I changed my attitude by overcoming my fear, and it changed my life.

I started getting feedback from key engineers, managers, and process and maintenance technicians. I did my best to get out into the process unit and out to the maintenance shop. I tried to learn every detail of the process, plant, herbicide business, and Monsanto as a whole. I also learned about people. I learned that relationships are incredibly valuable, and just as networking had gotten me a full-time job as a process engineer (or, in other words, got my foot in the door), I needed to build and nurture relationships while I was there to further my career and my net wealth. With that, I then took my boss's advice and tried to absorb Louisiana culture. I started a journal where I kept track of local sayings of Creole and Cajun French words (and yes, there is a difference between

Creole and Cajun). This would serve me well in building my social wealth with those from Louisiana then and in my future. Now, in my life, it's lagniappe (which means "a little something extra," like the 13th egg in a Baker's dozen) and a great way to connect with folks from Louisiana.

As the unit grew, my opportunities to grow as an engineer came as well. Over the next year from the fall of 1999 to the fall of 2000, I learned that what I had heard about engineering jobs was true: **"You spend the first year figuring out what is going on. The second year fixing all the stuff you did wrong the year before. And you spend the third year optimizing the work you did the previous two years."** Because I wasn't sure what I wanted to do long term and wasn't sure what advancement opportunities there were for me without a bachelor's degree, I put my head down and focused on building my financial wealth and financial intelligence (FI), which is **the ability of executives and employees to understand and execute on accounting principles.** Under this notion, executives and employees who aren't formally educated in finance or accounting still need to understand basic finance principles.

At that time, Monsanto had two tracks of advancement for engineers: management or technology. The highest level within the company for management was the Chief Executive Officer (CEO). The highest level within the company for technology was a manufacturing technologist (known within the company as MTs). Many managers had master's degrees, particularly MBAs. Many MTs had professional engineering (PE) licenses. I was drawn to the management track but was told I needed to progress from an entry-level engineer to an intermediate-level engineer and then make it to the senior engineering level before they'd decide what to do with me. I was told that would take at least two to four years.

I wasn't sure what to do. I wanted to go back to school because I wanted more job security, more career mobility, and the option to earn the MBA I had desired for so long. I also wanted to be debt-free, so I put my head down and did my best to advance as a process engineer in the DSIDA unit.

I had been assigned a role as the unit Environmental Compliance Officer (ECO), which put me in touch with other engineers and technicians throughout the plant. From 2000 to 2001 I really put a lot of effort into being an outstanding process engineer and ECO. I worked to build relationships with others throughout the plant. I also learned to maintain relationships with people after they left the plant, whether they stayed with Monsanto or not. In other words, I learned to better master **the art of networking**, which is critical to building social wealth.

This strategy paid off, and in the summer of 2001, my boss asked me if I would be interested in transferring to the plant environmental department as an environmental engineer. I had built a great rapport with the group. They had a vacancy coming up due to one of the engineer's upcoming maternity leave. I had been suggested as a replacement for her. At the time, I still wasn't sure if I was going to go into the management or technology track, and I still wanted to go back to school. One of the things I learned in those few years as a process engineer was that the programmers (also known as process control engineers) were the ones who REALLY ran the plant. They had to know EVERYTHING! They wrote the computer code that ran the computers that ran the chemical process. To me, THAT'S SMART!

At the time, a White female process control engineer from Cincinnati, OH, had been assigned to our unit to clean up some of the process code and institute improvements. She'd just come back from an international assignment in the startup of the

Monsanto Roundup® production plant in Camaçari, Brazil and she came HIGHLY recommended as a coder. I thought about the opportunity to learn from her and decided to turn down the environmental engineering position.

I stayed at DSIDA for another year (one year longer than the **"three-year rule of figure out, correct, optimize" career strategy I had learned**), but I developed a relationship with that engineer that I'll cherish for a lifetime. I also learned a lot that year, as she used to say, **"It's not what you say but how you say it!"** regarding the impact of communication on relationships, both professional and personal.

In the summer of 2002, my boss came to me with an offer AGAIN for a position as a plant environmental engineer. When he offered it to me, I was riding on a wave of positive feedback as a protegee of the female process control engineer. My boss told me to take the job as it would change my life...so I took it.

In August of 2002, I started my job as an environmental engineer at the Luling, LA Monsanto plant. Because of my previous role as ECO, the female environmental engineer that I was replacing and I had already built a rapport, so her showing me the ropes went well. The ropes included the responsibility of being the plant representative in the event of an international chemical weapons inspection. Little did I know that that one simple form was going to become so important so soon.

Crisis Management Skills

I was two weeks into my new job as an environmental engineer with responsibilities of representing the plant for the Monsanto company with the Organization for the Prohibition of Chemical Weapons (OPCW), when I got a fax from the United States State

Department. Our plant was first on the list for a chemical weapons audit from the OPCW, of which the United States is a part.

You must understand that at the time, the United States was in a tenuous international debate about chemical weapons inspections coming from the Middle East after the September 11 Terrorist Attacks. At the time, President George W. Bush was touting publicly that America was certain that Saddam Hussein had chemical weapons in his possession that he was storing in preparation to perpetuate an attack on the United States by Islamic countries. Our plant had been identified as a possible source to fuel a chemical attack on other countries by the United States, and here I was, the point of contact for all of this...and I was SHAKEN!

When I came to my boss with the fax, all I remember her telling me was, "I know you have a lot of balls in the air right now. Some of them are porcelain, some of them are rubber, and some of them are glass. Just don't drop any glass balls."

It didn't help that the plant was under a hurricane warning for Hurricane Isadore at the time. I needed to delicately tell the international community that we weren't open for inspection, all while considering the sensitive international situation. Hurricane Isadore was closely followed by Hurricane Lily, making things much more difficult. Nonetheless, both myself, the plant, and the country came out of the situation unscathed, and I came out promoted to intermediate engineer and was quickly becoming known for my crisis management skills.

Chapter 3

Part III

Knowledge Wealth:
Cracking Corporate Codes

My knowledge wealth EXPLODED from 2002 to 2004 when I worked as an environmental engineer. The explosion occurred because I was unconsciously aware of the five wealth currencies and their impact on total wealth. I found myself in a critical period in a woman's life. Her brain is fully developed, and her frontal lobe, which is fully developed, starts functioning fully as well. I spent my free time reinvesting in my FQ, IQ, and EQ.

In *Rich Dad Poor Dad: What the Rich Teach Their Kids About Money That the Poor and Middle Class Do Not!* by Robert Kiyosaki, I learned about the four cash flow quadrants and started to improve my FQ. Then I read *Cracking The Corporate Code: The Revealing Success Stories Of 32 African-American Executives* by Price M. Cobbs and Judith Turnock. In 2004 I read *Nice Girls Don't Get The Corner Office* by Lois Frankel and started implementing that knowledge in my workplace and started seeing results. I became a game-playing, micro messaging, insult-dodging, improvement-implementing BEAST! But how I did it is the most interesting factor.

You see, when I was transferred from DSIDA to the plant environmental department, I did so because they (the environmental department) liked my interest in environmental conservation. It happened to be at a time when I started exploring different wealth currencies, so I was open to more than just the financial gain of the position. I started to think about work-life balance, as HR professionals call it. With the pandemic of 2020 and the work-from-home revolution, many employers saw employees thinking more seriously about a work-wealth balance. All that being said, I found my new position as an environmental engineer a better fit for my life as a single mother, as I would no longer have to work nights and weekends without support from my family and leave my young son in the care of strangers.

After I was promoted to intermediate engineer (which my boss called "a seamless transition"), I immediately started asking what it would take for the next promotion. I was told that I needed to demonstrate the ability to lead a large-scale project that benefited the bottom line of the company. I found it difficult to identify a way I could lead a significant project since when I walked into most rooms at the company, I was the only Black, the only female, and (most of the time) the youngest person in the room. I had been given the lowest assignments on the totem pole when I joined the environmental department. That included now being the plant lead for chemical releases, which (according to the technicians) made me the police, not a good thing.

I had already been the DSIDA unit point of contact for releases when I was the ECO for the unit, so this was just the same role but on a larger scale. I spent each morning going through the chemical releases for the plant from the previous day and entering the data into a Microsoft Access database. Just a few weeks after I started entering the data into the database, I thought, *this is stupid! Why am I entering this data for all the technicians and engineers in the plant? They should be doing this themselves.* That is when the idea hit me for web-based release reporting.

Project Management Skills: 2002-2005

When I took on the role of plant ECO coordinator, I felt like it was a promotion. I had essentially gone from ECO coordinator to plant ECO lead. While it felt good, I wasn't thrilled with my new position as a plant environmental engineer, so I decided to make the best of it. I found that as a Black female engineer, my voice didn't have as much weight in rooms as the voices of my White male counterparts. I didn't know how to stand out, but I thought that with this web-based release reporting project, I might get the attention for my skills that I so desired.

I went to my boss (the Black female that had originally hired me) with my idea. A web-based release reporting system that was available to any plant employee at any time. They could go to an internal web page and enter the amount of the release based on the part of the system that had the release. It would be immediately reported through the plant release system, including a page (yeah, it was the early 2000s) to the plant environmental engineer on call. What I had in mind would make me a BEAST! I moved forward with my plan to implement web-based release reporting to the Monsanto Luling, LA plant.

The idea was a hit! When I shared my idea with the other ECOs, they were ecstatic. No longer would they have to worry about whether their calculations of chemical releases would be correct, but they would have the immediate support they so

85

desperately desired in dealing with release situations. That's when I realized information was a source of power that was more valuable than money. **It's not just what you know but who you know and what you know about who you know and what who you know knows about you.**

It reminded me of the movie *Sneakers* starring Robert Redford and Sydney Poitier (which I HIGHLY recommend watching in this new digital age). There is a point when a third character (the villain) says to Robert Redford's character, "It's about the information, Marty!"

Some units were calculating releases with an Excel spreadsheet. Some were using a calculator. All I knew was that these people needed help...and FAST! My boss told me to find out from the IT department what it would take and how much it would cost to build and maintain. I went to the head of the IT department and shared the idea with him. He told me he would get back to me on how much it would cost and who would be assigned to the project. He later came back to me and hit me with a ton of bricks. It would cost us NOTHING! He assigned the project to an IT department programmer who needed to learn how to code in Pearl and Oracle (which would be the database we'd use) and how to link it to the existing Microsoft Access database that the environmental department was already using. My knowledge of coding in Access from building my own music database seven years earlier at night while my child was asleep while I interned in Iowa made me the perfect lead for this project.

It took countless hours over the next two years for me and the IT coder to build the web-based release reporting system. I demonstrated the ability to lead a large plant project and improved release reporting sitewide. Just one month after the site launched, we saw an over 2000% increase in releases reported. The project was a complete success! I spent the next year working out the bugs and improving the system. I was asked to present the project at a plant safety meeting. My presentation went so well, and the project was so successful that it was selected to represent the Luling, LA plant for the 2005 Monsanto Manufacturing, Environmental, Safety, & Health (MESH) Global Corporate Conference. Initially, I was asked to present the project by speaking live at the conference, but in the end, I was downgraded to a poster. Nonetheless, I did end up meeting the CEO of Monsanto at the time (Hugh Grant) and he loved my project! He even asked if there was a way to implement it globally throughout the company!

I went back to Louisiana and promptly asked my temporary boss for a transfer to another plant as soon as possible. For social wealth reasons, I needed to leave the state. I had also been told that if I wanted to be a corporate environmental manager, I needed additional plant experience in a different location, and I needed to be promoted to senior engineer first. What I was being told was something new and different. You see, everyone within Monsanto was on a development plan, but only a few select people were on a succession plan. What I was being told was how to get on a succession plan, and I liked it. A succession plan meant you were on track to move up in the company based on your performance in your given role.

A plant staff coworker and friend from Brazil even asked me if I wanted to come and work for her. While it would be a high-profile position because she was the business unit leader for all of glyphosate intermediate production at the plant, I declined because I was learning how succession planning worked, and I knew she was probably going to hire someone that I didn't need to end up working for since we had a long personal history. I would be reporting to him as an area planner (a step up for me) and he would be the unit supervisor.

Hurricane Katrina – Crisis Management Skills 2005-2006

While I was on the company's radar for a succession plan, I started being considered for positions at other locations. At the same time, my web-based release reporting project, along with a co-worker's Six Sigma project on releases, were selected for a Louisiana Governor's Environmental Leadership award. Shortly after that, Hurricane Katrina hit Louisiana, and all hell broke loose.

The plant saw three feet of flooding, and there were large chemical releases that had to be cleaned up. When I went back to the plant two weeks after the storm, Luling was one of the few places that had power. As soon as I got back to work, I went to my new boss's office, slammed the door shut and yelled, "When am I getting a transfer?!" He was stunned and responded that he thought I was coming in to resign since I had my son enrolled in school in Florida. All the schools in the Louisiana area had been closed due to the storm. I told him I wanted a transfer, a raise, and a promotion since I felt I had more than demonstrated the abilities of a senior-level engineer. I had learned to **ask for what I wanted.**

While he agreed he had seen I had done a wonderful job over the last three years, the plant staff felt that I lacked experience in the air environmental medium from a technical perspective. He also thought I wanted a transfer because things were so chaotic after the hurricane. I told him I had requested the transfer from my temporary boss in May, long before the storm. He asked me if I was willing to help get the plant up and running, and he would get back to me on the transfer. I agreed to stay. I worked twelve to fourteen hours a day, seven days a week, for at least a month. He checked with my temporary boss, who confirmed that I had requested the transfer long before the storm hit. My boss agreed to advocate for me finding a position at another location somewhere else within the company. He told me to feel free to start looking at the internal listings on the corporate job website.

I continued to work as well as volunteering to help other employees whose houses were flooded. A group of us were suffering from what is called survivor's guilt, and helping those employees gut their houses was a healthy way to cope with it. Later, in the fall of 2005, a position opened at the Augusta, GA facility and my boss mentioned it to me to see if I was interested. I knew the engineer who had been dismissed from the position, so I already had a rather good idea of what I would be dealing with. My boss discouraged me from applying for the position as it was an ESH position that would give me minimal air environmental media experience. A few months later, in the spring of 2006, a position opened up at the Muscatine facility. My boss encouraged me to apply, and I did. When I went to the interview, I was told that it was essentially up to me whether I wanted the position or not. It would come with a 3% pay raise and all relocation expenses covered. Because I had come to understand what it meant to be on a succession plan, I took the position.

Muscatine, IA 2006-2009

For various health wealth reasons, much of the professional work I did at the Muscatine plant is a blur to me at this point in my life because I allowed a White male environmental engineer to dump his personal problems on me in my office on a regular basis. I hadn't yet learned how to emotionally protect myself at work. I do remember that I was transferred there with the hope that I would implement my web-based release reporting project at that plant, but I never did. I thought I would end up spending more time doing administrative work instead of building relationships and developing my technical skills as an environmental engineer with air medium experience. I did, however, participate in the global Six Sigma release reporting project with the lead team (including me) meeting in Antwerp, Belgium, in June of 2008. While in Muscatine, I was also assigned the Title V air permit renewal, which included regular submissions of EIQ reporting to the Iowa Department of Natural Resources (IDNR). I submitted it, but a White male senior environmental engineer in the department found errors in my submission. I was put on a corrective action plan in the summer of 2008. I was terminated from my environmental engineering position in January of 2009 with a severance package including three months' salary and full relocation benefits anywhere in the lower forty-eight United States.

I quickly learned what it was like to be unemployed. I applied for unemployment through the state of Iowa and immediately started looking for a new job. I found a position with Edward Jones and thought it might be a good fit. I loved personal finance, so I thought it would be a good way for me to pivot in my career. The position paid just above minimum wage during training, and they paid for all of the licensing exams. It was an opportunity for me to get my Series 7 license and would allow me to trade stock options for other people at a profit. I accepted the position of financial advisor with Edward Jones in April 2009. I started studying for my Series 7, Series 66, and 2-15 licenses while preparing to relocate to Orlando, FL.

That season in my life was also a time when I had to really exercise skills in frugality and demonstrate that I understood that **"When you watch the pennies, the dollars take care of themselves."** Thankfully, I had built a financial war chest, especially for times like this. I sold my Monsanto corporate stock options to pay for my wedding to my current husband, which was my splurge for 2009, which was also when I turned thirty-five years old.

My first marriage taught me one of the most critical things in life: **"Who you marry is one of the biggest wealth decisions you will ever make in your life."**

After my divorce, I knew that IF I married again, it would be for life. I knew that I would be more careful in my selection of a life partner, and I knew his finances would need to be in order, or we'd not be a good fit for one another. I had read *Date or Soul Mate?: How to Know If Someone Is Worth Pursuing in Two Dates or Less* by Neil Clark Warren (a gift from a Luling male coworker), so I had my list of top five must-haves and top five can't-stands. I put my money where my mouth was and when I did get married again, I paid for the entire wedding. It was my last financial act as a single woman.

In the fall of 2010, I returned to Tallahassee to complete my Bachelor of Science degree in Chemical Engineering. According to my academic advisor, I was 32 credit hours shy of the degree, and it would take me about three semesters to complete it. After two weeks, I had to withdraw for health reasons and move back to Orlando. I started researching online chemical engineering degree programs and came across one at the University of North Dakota. The entire program could be done online, with labs completed in person in North Dakota during the summer months. The only problem was all my chemical engineering credits wouldn't transfer, and I would have to spend two years in their program for a total of six semesters before I could graduate. I went ahead and enrolled and started the program in January 2011.

About two weeks into classes, my husband came home and asked how things were going. I was overwhelmed and struggling to recall the math required to do chemical engineering. He asked

91

me how much the program was going to cost and I told him $80,000 because of the out-of-state tuition fees. He was taken aback. Two years of my life and $80,000 of student loans just to get a bachelor's degree in chemical engineering so I could go on and get my MBA just didn't make sense to him. He suggested I investigate getting a bachelor's degree in business. He had graduated from the University of Central Florida with his BS in mechanical engineering, so he knew it was a solid program. In addition, I could go to classes in person and still live at home. I applied but was declined.

I did some more research and found that the University of Florida (UF) had a completely online Bachelor of Business Administration (BSBA) program. I decided to apply and was conditionally accepted. There were a few prerequisite business courses I would need to complete at the local community college before I could transfer to UF's program. I withdrew from UND and enrolled at Valencia Community College in the summer of 2011. I was taking Introduction to Accounting, and I was excited about starting my own business and told my professor so. He said, "That's great. Do you know what your break-even is yet?" I hadn't done that research, so I took that question and got to work. I also studied for and obtained my Florida state real estate sales associate license. My husband's job at the Kennedy Space Center ended, and he started working full-time in the property management business. I quickly saw that he needed help. One key knowledge wealth coin I learned is that **when you are married, you are partners, and you need to work together to accomplish shared goals.** While my husband is an incredibly smart person, between the two of us, I have stronger organizational and planning skills. This presented a problem with him leading our business, so I stepped in to assist.

I took on the title of business manager and went about building the business. I learned how the property management software worked and became the go-to person for computer issues in the office. I developed my sales skills by reeling in one lead after another. The franchisors and my husband were all impressed with my sales skills. I also took over the finances for the office. I tracked the income and expenses, the bills, our fees, etc. I forecasted and kept a close eye on the profit and loss statements, the balance sheets, and all other aspects of the business. I became painfully familiar with 1099 tax reporting procedures for rental property owners and property management companies, all while going to school.

We also learned a valuable lesson with the purchase of an Infiniti I35 in September 2011. My husband wanted a new car to go with the new business and talked me into buying a used 2009 car. Not one week after we purchased it, it broke down. We had it towed to an AAMCO franchise location. We weren't sure what was wrong with it, but it seemed to be electrical. When the mechanic came back to us and told us we needed a new transmission, and it was going to be $5k, we were floored.

Given that we had just started our new property management business, we sucked it up and charged the new transmission on our American Express card. We happily drove off, thinking everything was fine. Then it happened. A few weeks later, we were driving back to Orlando from Brevard County on 528 when the car broke down...again. Thankfully, we had recently changed car insurance coverage and had unlimited towing because we ended up having that car towed nine times over five weeks. Eventually, we took the car to the local dealer who gave us a loaner vehicle while they troubleshot our vehicle. It took them a month, but they eventually found a short in the instrument panel. We disputed the transmission charge with American Express and won! **That is a lesson in the power of using credit cards for major purchases.**

In January 2012 I started the online BSBA business program with the University of Florida. I greatly enjoyed the prerequisites I had taken at the community college and found that the timing of classes and starting our business was seamless. I had a real-world opportunity to apply everything I was learning in the classroom, and I found it quite satisfying. I continued with the degree program while working in the property management business full-time. Just two months before graduation in 2014, I noticed that something didn't look right in the rental escrow bank register. While I had noticed the balance going down each month, now it was negative, and I didn't think the software would allow that. I called the franchise corporate office for assistance. What happened after that rocked my world.

After much investigation, our corporate support person found that we had been overpaying the owner for a year and that the funds had been coming out of the rental escrow account. Because the owner had a significant number of properties, the problem was magnified to the point we had overpaid her around $50,000. The problem was no longer a problem; it was a crisis. The franchise owner got involved and contacted the software company that we used to manage our business. After several rounds with them, they admitted there was a glitch in their system that allowed overpayment to happen, but they weren't taking any financial responsibility for the issue. We were going to have to go to the owner, tell her what happened, and ask for our money back. There are a lot of times in life when it's difficult to communicate with someone and this was going to be one of the most difficult phone calls I had ever had to make in my life.

I braced myself as I dialed her number. How was I going to explain such an egregious error? I was supposed to be financially savvy. How could I miss this? She answered, and I told her the situation. She was shocked. She was dismayed. She was livid. She didn't have $50,000 just sitting around for her to send to us.

When she'd started receiving income from the properties she'd inherited, she quit her job and enrolled in school full-time to get the education she needed to pursue her dream job. The yelling that followed was excruciating. I realized I was in over my head and got the franchisor on the phone with the owner. Things still didn't go well. In the end, the franchisor worked out an agreement with the owner where we'd make the correction in the software and pull funds from her disbursement each month until the balance was paid back. We'd pay her a minimum of $4,000 for the first few months so she would have enough to live on. In addition, our office would eat $1,000 toward the balance each month until the balance was fully repaid. It was a painful and expensive but valuable lesson that came just as I finished my BSBA at the University of Florida in August 2014.

I continued to work in the business for another year while I started squirreling away money again now that we had income. In the spring of 2016, my husband's best friend shared with us that he and his wife were opening another All County property management office, but this time, they were going to do so in Jacksonville, FL. Because it's my hometown and they knew I was originally interested in that territory, they asked us if we'd be interested in partnering with them in the new venture. I loved the idea! The passive income was a great fit for the cash flow strategy we were working toward. While we were only buying 20% of the office ownership, I poured a lot of sweat equity into the startup of the business. I transitioned out of day-to-day operations at the end of 2016.

Over the next couple of years, I learned how to balance running multiple businesses (with my spouse, might I add) and manage our own rental property, all while being a wife and mother of a young child. In the summer of 2018, I reached my limit. I wasn't making progress toward my MBA, and I had grown tired of the property management business. I wanted to spend more time on personal finance and working at All County just wasn't doing it for me anymore. I decided it was time to go back to school...again. In the fall of 2018, I applied for the University of Florida's professional MBA program. The curriculum was delivered in person with one week for foundations review. While I wasn't thrilled with the $40,000 in student loans that it cost me, the education has been INVALUABLE to my knowledge wealth.

In the spring of 2019, I was enrolled in corporate finance, managerial quantitative analysis, and professional writing classes. For summer 2019 I was enrolled in risk and crisis management as well as a negotiations class. In the fall of 2019, I enrolled in a customer insights class, a professional communication class, and an international business class. I also had the opportunity to participate in UF's international MBA immersion program. In the fall of the same year, I spent a week in Brazil (both in Rio and Sao Paolo), learning about business operations in their country. From there, I enrolled in global strategic management and customer relationship management classes.

The pandemic that hit in late winter/early spring of 2020 was a test I hadn't prepared for in any way. I found myself scouring the internet for information and watching the news nonstop. I kept wondering how this crisis was going to affect the global economy. I was relieved when Congress passed the paycheck protection program. It allowed me to focus on my new career as an agent for a top life insurance company. In the spring of 2020, I passed my 2-15 Life, Health, and Variable Annuities licensing exam.

The life insurance industry, in my opinion, is very much like a pyramid scheme in that the company must keep signing people up for policies to keep the company profitable. Life insurance sales is also much like a dog fight. The competition was fierce, and leadership had no problem pitting one agent against another. Leadership, from my perspective, also didn't seem to be concerned about the financial welfare of their insured. I know whole life insurance has gotten a bad rap among many financial gurus, including Suze Orman, Dave Ramsey, and Primerica, but because I've learned so much about how it can be used as a retirement and tax planning tool, I have a different opinion of it now. I've read *The Power Of Zero* by David McKnight, so I'm keenly familiar with life insurance retirement planning (LIRP) as a strategy to avoid future tax increases effects on retirement balances in the long run. I also read *What Would The Rockefellers Do?* by Garrett B. Gunderson, so I had a good understanding of how to set up a family bank account using whole life insurance.

The following is an image I used while selling whole life insurance to convince people to purchase it in an effort to avoid and plan for upcoming tax increases.

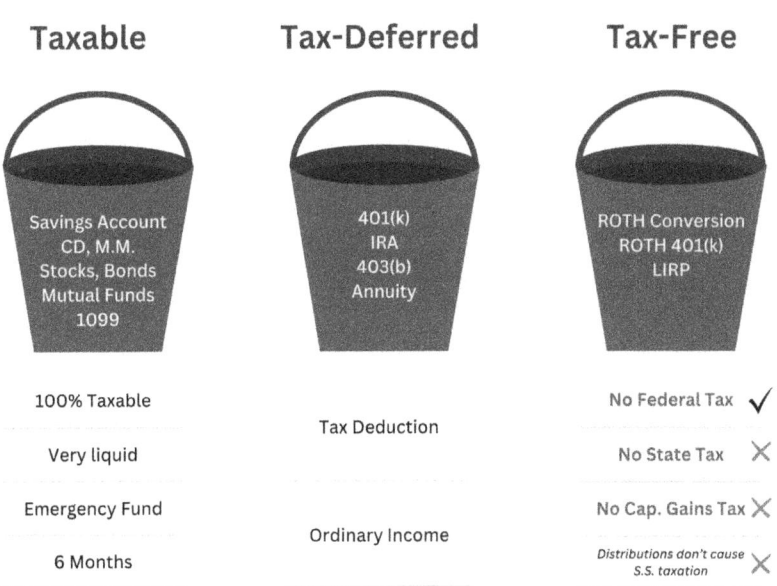

Taxable	Tax-Deferred	Tax-Free
Savings Account CD, M.M. Stocks, Bonds Mutual Funds 1099	401(k) IRA 403(b) Annuity	ROTH Conversion ROTH 401(k) LIRP
100% Taxable		No Federal Tax ✓
	Tax Deduction	
Very liquid		No State Tax ✗
Emergency Fund		No Cap. Gains Tax ✗
	Ordinary Income	
6 Months		*Distributions don't cause S.S. taxation* ✗

What I learned was that those popular financial gurus were only partially right. Yes, we should be investing in our 401(k)s and 403(b)s, but contributing to them up to the federal limit (also known as maxing it out) is usually NOT the best strategy first. Minimizing bad debt is the first step to financial freedom. After bad debt elimination, saving for emergencies should be next. While that bucket is being filled, I believe people should take advantage of tax-deferred savings accounts like 401(k)s and 403(b)s, especially if there is an employer match to the employee contribution, as it gives the investor 100% return on their investment. I also believe people should invest in a Roth IRA up to the federal limit each year as much as possible BEFORE they start putting funds into a LIRP. This is where I found the most conflict as an insurance agent. Pushing whole life insurance as the main product, even when term life insurance made more sense from a holistic wealth perspective, was the norm at the company.

In April 2021, things became so tense in the insurance game for me that my boss asked me to resign. I declined. While we didn't need the income, the job was worth holding onto for the health insurance benefits alone. On our own, health insurance costs more than the mortgage on our rental property, so keeping health insurance benefits was critical to our financial strategy. I stayed on while my husband and I tried to figure out what else I could do.

In the fall of 2021, I learned how cold and unfeeling an insurance employer can be. I had a client who purchased a whole life insurance policy for his business. Unbeknownst to me, the client's payment bounced, and the company reversed my commission and canceled my health insurance. I didn't discover this until October 2021 when I tried to refill an outstanding expensive prescription for a serious chronic illness. My direct supervisor (who was aware of my health situation), nor the head of the regional office were of little to no assistance. Due to significant health issues that were impacting my household's finances, I did my best to hold on to the job even though I should've known better. I mean, the company is driven by a bunch of actuaries, and I was given a specialized pre-employment test and then told they had never seen anyone score that high before. My boss literally told me I was "a unicorn."

I did everything I was told to do to try to reinstate my health insurance all to no avail, so I decided to shank them with my "unicorn" horn. In January 2022, I resigned from my position and hired an attorney to recover damages and medical expenses for the healthcare I required after my health insurance was terminated.

The experience proved the adage **people don't quit companies; people quit people** to be true. If I were offered a position with the company again, it wouldn't be as a whole life insurance agent or "financial advisor." I would find more joy in improving my knowledge base by pursuing a PhD in business.

While I had been enjoying the fact-finding part of being a life insurance agent and had found great joy in teaching financial literacy to people, I decided it was time to work for the one person who would be the most challenging for me...myself. And I was going to use everything I had learned about people, relationships, and emotional intelligence to capitalize on my social wealth.

That's when I started Lighthouse Wealth Coaching, a holistic wealth business focused on creating generational wealth.

Chapter 4

Part I

Social Wealth: Starts at Home

When we're born, we come into a foundation of social wealth through our family of origin (the family into which we're born). Social wealth (sometimes referred to as social capital), according to The Social Capital Group, an accredited investor's group of which I'm a member, is "**linked to social networks, particularly those where members have a sufficient level of trust for network members to communicate effectively and provide each other with valuable resources.**" It's also been known as one's sphere of influence.

As we go through life, we build our social wealth through relationships with others that we encounter along the way. A dear friend, Cynthia James, around 1999, shared her perspective of me and the meaning of my name, and I share it as an example of how social wealth impacts those who know you and determines your wealth in their life. Cynthia wrote:

"Njeri- of or belonging to a warrior; a warrior or fighter. Strong, fiery, clever, determined and talented – a few of the characteristics that personify your name. Beautiful, exquisite, passionate, caring and loyal – a few of the characteristics that make you special but also leave you vulnerable. Candid, honest, mysterious, graceful and spiritual – a few of the qualities that make you interesting and keep you grounded. One of a kind, a work of art, unique, funny, yet poignant are a few of the characteristics that make you a master-piece and make you priceless.

One of the best things about you is your incredible strength and ability to endure through all the tough times. I admire you most for your honesty. I treasure you most for your friendship. I love you most because you are you. What I want most for you is for you to know God because only He can offer the unconditional love you crave. Only then will you be able to give and accept this love to and from yourself and others. I pray that you realize and reach your full potential."

I love her words. They remain framed in my closet. I have to admit, though, that I still don't feel I have the strongest social skills, and I definitely have more work to do on my emotional intelligence. But her words encourage me.

A lot of that social and emotional intelligence lack comes from my sheltered childhood. The people I have either encountered or built relationships with while living with my parents affected my holistic social wealth in those formative years.

When I turned five my mother missed my birthday to go to my dad's village to get one of my male cousins and bring him to the U.S. as our newly adopted brother. The moment he joined our family, I immediately noticed that my father treated our new brother differently than me and my sisters. When I came home from school with my sisters the day they returned, my father was helping him learn how to ride a bike, and not just any bike, MY BIKE!

My father had always wanted a son to carry on the Gichia family name. Because my Cesarian birth nearly killed my mother, she had to have an emergency hysterectomy. I was sent to foster care for two and a half months. When I got out of foster care, my parents decided to change my name from Frances (after my father) to Njeri. I was the only one of my sisters with a Kikuyu first and last name, which brought me closer to my father until the new brother came along.

My father's friend (Uncle Kagombe) invited us all to the UN for New Year's Eve in 1979. I remember walking across the street with all the cars and taxis and the honking horns. I remember the room with all the tables with different flags on them. I remember hearing all the different languages and feeling so at home. There happened to be a flower on the table next to ours, and I wanted it. My parents encouraged me to go over and ask for it from the diplomat. I was nervous. I was five! At the end of the night, I took a deep breath and mustered up all the courage in my little body, walked over to the table and asked for the flower. The diplomat was so impressed with me (and thought I was kind of cute) and happily gave me the flower. From what I am told, I took the flower, and my face lit up! Ever since then, I have dreamed of returning to the United Nations.

I have also made it a point to try to get to know people from as many different cultures and countries as possible so I can expand my social wealth. I have often dreamed of living overseas as an ex-pat at some point in my career and I still don't rule it out as a possibility. I have even started researching another country to retire to considering the MIT study published in 1972 forecasting the global collapse of society around 2040.

My dad also had a friend called Uncle Waiguchu. He and his wife, who we called Tata (which is Kikuyu for Aunt) Njeri had a daughter named Lisa. They were my third sister's godparents, and Uncle Waiguchu was a professor at a local college. His friendship with my father reinforced the value of higher education for me. Later, Tata Njeri's business ventures piqued my interest.

A significant part of my social wealth has been affected by both my gender and my race, neither of which I had any control over. My parents were my first source of social wealth. Both being first-generation college graduates, they greatly valued higher level education, a value they also instilled in me. Over time, they also planted seeds for spiritual wealth (which is connected to social wealth), which showed up from them in my formative years as religion.

Since my father had been indoctrinated as Anglican when the British came and colonized Kenya, one church we tried was San Jose Episcopal. It was predominantly White and on the "White side of town" 15 minutes from our home. After one service, it was clear we weren't welcome, so my parents looked for another church. They found an all-Black Episcopal church in downtown Jacksonville called St. Phillips Episcopal Church. It was over a 30-minute drive, but we made it our church home. We only attended on Christmas and Easter until my oldest sister was eligible for marriage in 1985. Then, we started attending weekly. We developed a bond with Father Angus, who was from Jamaica and led the parishioners of our church.

I learned over the years that I had a lot in common with people from the Caribbean, like the relationship I had with Africans. I was exposed to Africans a lot while I was growing up because my father was from Kenya. My mother is an introvert, so she didn't have many friends and my dad's friends were mostly who I was exposed to socially while growing up. My mother was friendly with my father's friends' wives, but I only remember her meeting with one of her own friends. It was a White woman with a son about my age. She was a midwife like my mother, but she had her own practice. She was a single mother when we met up with her and her son in Nairobi, Kenya, in the summer of 1983.

Around that same time, I joined a local Girl Scouts chapter, thanks to a girl with whom I went to elementary school. Her name was Erin O'Neal, but everyone called her by her middle name, Kelly. Her parents' house was one of the few houses I was allowed to go to for sleepovers, as my parents were incredibly strict and conservative. I learned that people in different houses do things differently.

I was driven to earn as many patches as possible while I was in the Girl Scouts. I was driven to succeed in the annual cookie sales as well. I did some door-to-door sales as well as sales outside of grocery stores, but I was an innovator in business even then. I made most of my sales by sending my sheets to school with two of my older sisters who were in high school. Their classmates didn't have many younger siblings, so they didn't have as much access to those coveted Girl Scout cookies. I had my sisters work with me on sales and delivery, and I won the most sales in my troop that year.

In fifth grade (right before my 10th birthday), a TV movie based on a true story titled *The Burning Bed* starring Farrah Fawcett was on NBC one night. My mother made me watch it, and I was captivated. The story is about a poor mother of three who is physically abused by her husband. If I remember correctly, she tries to get an education and get a job so she can be financially independent from her husband, and he beats her for that and so many other things. Eventually, she loses it and kills him one night after he has beaten and raped her then passed out drunk on their bed. In a state of temporary insanity, she sets the bed on fire with him in it, takes the children, and leaves. I think she was exonerated, but the message I got was to **always have your own income as a woman and never tolerate abuse from a man**. This also left me sensitive to maintaining as much of my independence as possible for as long as possible.

Even though I had made friends with some of the White girls in my neighborhood, the parents were iffy about us. Our immediate neighbors on both sides were Jewish. Facing East, the old woman to our right never spoke to us, and the original family to our left were conservative Jews. I learned early about Jewish culture and the religion from our neighbors. They would even walk up the street to the temple near our home every Saturday.

The neighborhood was about half Jewish, and we'd see them walking on Saturdays. There was a significant Jewish population in the public schools as well, and I noticed when they were absent for the Jewish holidays Rosh Shoshana and Yom Kippur. After the neighbors to the left moved out (he was a doctor, and she was a housewife with two kids), a new family moved in with their two children. They were also Jewish, and the husband was a doctor as well. My sister would babysit for them on some weekends for extra money. I would play with their daughter, who was just a little younger than me.

One afternoon, she and I were playing in her house with another White girl from a few doors down. No parents were around to supervise us (we were Gen X kids), but the next-door neighbor girl and I never left her bedroom. On the other hand, the other girl was all over the house. I recall shortly after that play date, the next-door neighbors came to my parents and suggested that either my sister or I had stolen the wife's necklace. Now, neither my sister nor I are thieves, so my parents were insulted and told them it wasn't possible that their daughters had stolen anything. Things got so heated that both my sister and I sat through lie detector tests in an attorney's office to prove that we were telling the truth. My test came back with an ambiguous result on one question. Did I know of anyone who was alone in their parents' bedroom? I didn't know if the other girl had been in their room, and I had not seen her steal the necklace, but I knew she wasn't in the kids' rooms playing with us. Later the necklace was found in the other girl's bedroom at her house. Our family never got an apology.

Our whole family traveled to Kenya in the summer of 1983. We'd return home, however, without our adopted brother. He had been causing a lot of problems both at home and at school from when he first arrived. Ultimately, he wanted to be sent back to Africa, and he got his wish. When we returned to the US and were having our usual family dinner my father mentioned a cousin coming to live with us while she went to university. We had stayed with her family (Uncle Munoru and Tata Sarah) while we were in Kenya that summer. Their youngest daughter and I were agemates and wrote letters to each other over the years to stay in touch. The only problem with her sister coming to live with us was that our family needed to heal from the disruptions of the males who had been living with us and causing so many issues; my father was clearly a chauvinist (or, at the very least, very African).

I distinctly remember speaking up at the dinner table, sharing that thought with my parents and then following with, "It's hard to see the picture when you are inside the frame." They were stunned at my insight, but my cousin came to live with us anyway. The culture clash was unbearable, and I can't remember when, but she eventually moved out. From there, it was a revolving door of African relatives coming to live with us, including Kagombe's only daughter, with whom I always corresponded as we too were agemates.

She and I had grown up writing letters to each other on the old blue airmail sheets. Later, while I was in middle school, my father allowed another of my cousins to come and live with us. My mother had watched my father send money to Kenya over the years, and it was a point of conflict because Africans are known for their corruption. My cousin was no exception. When he tried to talk my father into investing a significant amount of money in his new business in South Florida as a way of moving out, I vehemently told my father not to do it as I knew he would never see the money again. Unfortunately, I was right. That was just one example in life of learning by watching other people's experiences.

When my second sister graduated from high school in 1986, my parents made a BIG DEAL out of it because she would be the first to go away to college. She was to study Accounting at The University of Florida in nearby Gainesville, where my mother was going to complete her PhD in Nursing with a minor in Cultural Anthropology. There had to be at least seventy to eighty people at our home to celebrate her graduation. We even killed a goat! Killing a goat is customary for celebrations in Kikuyu culture. I got to go with my father to the butcher to pick it up. It's something I will never forget, especially since there was no such celebration when I graduated from high school with honors and a full scholarship.

He wasn't the last of my father's side of the family to come and live with us. When we moved to Florida, my cousin Stephen Kamau came from France after completing his degree in computer science. He was supposed to get an advanced degree while he was living with us, but a short time later, he moved to Miami and started doing computer work as an independent contractor. Luther Campbell (also known as Uncle Luke of the notorious rap group 2 Live Crew) was one of his clients.

My cousin visited our home in Jacksonville in mid-1986 and played an unreleased 12" vinyl record in our playroom while my mom was sewing my sister's wedding dress. What did we hear on that record? *Boom. Boom. Boom Boom Boom.* "Somebody say, 'HEY WE WANT SOME P*SSY!'" My mother turned red from the neck up and she dropped everything and walked out of the room. I was 12. To me, this is a great example of social wealth for Generation X.

Later, there would be a huge legal debate nationally about free speech and 2 Live Crew was right at the center of it. When Bruce Springsteen allowed 2 Live Crew to sample his hit "Born In The USA" for their single "Banned In The USA," I watched the power of social wealth make a significant impact. I watched America be what the founders thought of, even in their humanity. If Bruce Springsteen (who was the whitest of the White rock stars of the time) could stand with a Black rap group to further free speech, then there was hope for me to do the same in my future.

In sixth grade, I was enrolled in school at the R.V. Daniels Sixth Grade Center, which was on the Black side of town (so I was bused from my White neighborhood to desegregate the schools). After I started puberty, I befriended two bad White girls. I started bringing alcohol to school on the school bus, and the other girls would bring cigarettes. We'd sit at the back of the bus on the way home and get lit. After a while, we also became bullies. We beat up a couple of kids for their candy. Eventually, one of the kids squealed, and one morning, when I arrived at school, I was escorted directly to the principal's office.

Mrs. Josephine Fiveashe sat me down and told me that someone had reported that me and a couple of other students were smoking and drinking alcohol on the school bus. She asked me if this was true. I thought carefully about what I had learned up to that point about being a woman, and I knew that I had to tell the truth and take responsibility for my actions, so I boldly replied, "Yes." She said she was going to call my mother immediately and I said, "Fine," since I just knew my mother was still at work and wouldn't answer the phone. Not only that, but I would also arrive home before her and be able to delete the answering machine message. Imagine my surprise when my mother answered.

She was livid and shocked. She asked me where I was getting the alcohol, and I told her from the six-pack of beer that Uncle Smiley (one of my dad's African cousins) had left on his last visit. The principal said according to the Duval County Student Code of Conduct, I was supposed to be expelled for one year and one day, but because I told the truth they were going to send me to the guidance counselor.

Once a week, I went to the neighboring sixth grade center at Susie Tolbert Elementary for gifted classes. Those students were being bused in from another White side of town. There weren't enough gifted students at each school, so the students were pooled into one classroom. While in that gifted class, I met a little White boy named Rick Hill. Although Rick and I came from two completely different sides of town, our similar interests in learning and politics were the foundation of our friendship, which may never have occurred if it weren't for desegregation. I would continue through school with Rick in seventh and eighth grade at Stanton and again in 11th and 12th grade at Stanton.

Rick and I had learned a lot in AP American History with our teacher, Mr. Steve Piscitelli, and had some interesting debates about racism and politics in the U.S. It was in Mr. Piscitelli's (we all called him Mr. P) class that I learned the definition of chattel. Mr. P was notorious for using a rubber chicken to teach his class.

Between classes, he would stand outside his classroom with the rubber chicken in his hand, greeting the students as they walked through the hall.

During his class, he would use the rubber chicken as a pointer. Then he got to the part about slavery and chattel in the American Constitution. He asked us if we knew what it meant to be chattel. My seat was at the very back of the classroom in the corner, so I was shocked when the rubber chicken flew past me and hit the wall behind me. After that, Mr. P said that being chattel meant the owner could do whatever he wanted with the slaves, including kill them. That struck me.

In our senior year at Stanton, Rick and I were in AP European History with our teacher, Mr. Garland Rushing. That year Mr. Rushing offered to be the school sponsor for our after-school club called Young Americans for Freedom. We had to name it that because it was a public school, and we couldn't call it what we wanted to call it –The Young Republicans Club. I wasn't old enough to vote yet, but I liked President Reagan, and I considered myself a conservative, so I chose to spend some of my free time exploring those ideas. In that club, I made a lot of social connections that were reestablished through Facebook and LinkedIn decades later which helped propel my and my husband's wealth. Both social media apps have been instrumental in increasing my social wealth over the years by improving my social capital.

I reconnected with high school classmate Bonnie Hall through Facebook when she and her family moved to Orlando. Given that she and her husband, Matthew Bradshaw, who are both engineers like my husband and I, we get along well with them, and we enjoyed being their Realtors® in their home buying process. We had a lot in common as teens (Bonnie and I), and I never forgot how she was the only person to attend my Sweet Sixteen party.

Stanton was historically a Black school on the Black side of town in downtown Jacksonville. It was changed into an integrated college preparatory magnet school for 7-12 grade public school students in the early '80s. My parents were disappointed that my older sisters just missed the entrance opportunity but pushed for me to get in, which I did.

The bus rides to and from Stanton were long. Again, since I lived on the White side of town, I rarely saw other Black kids on the ride home. In fact, there were only two on my school bus in seventh grade: a junior named Chuck Nearon and another seventh-grade girl named Cindy Workcuff. She and I became fast friends. She was disappointed when I left Stanton after eighth grade. I had applied to return to Stanton in 10th grade after being terribly bullied by the Black girls after school for a month in ninth grade at duPont. I was literally beaten because I had a weave in my hair, and that wasn't acceptable back then in the Black community. I was denied reentry into Stanton. When I got the rejection letter, I broke down in tears. I was suffering socially at the neighborhood school even though I was in advanced classes.

When I arrived at Wolfson for 10th grade, I hoped that I would become part of an accepted group. I had tried out for the sophomore junior varsity all-female cheerleading team and was their first pick. My mother refused to support me in being a cheerleader because she thought the uniforms were too revealing. On the first day of that school year, I walked into the lunchroom and recognized everyone was already established in their cliques.

My social anxiety was so overwhelming that I just walked out, found a hallway on the other side of the school, and sat there alone studying through lunch. I did that every day through my sophomore year. I spent that summer during the day in summer school at the newly built Mandarin High School but was elated when

Cindy and I both ended up in AP American History together in 11th grade. Then, I got a call at home on Labor Day that I was readmitted to Stanton. It wasn't until years later that I found out my mother's social wealth was why I was readmitted. She saw that I was really trying to do well in school and made a phone call to someone she knew and convinced them to let me back in. Even though I left Mandarin to go back to Stanton for my junior year in high school, it wasn't the last I would see of Cindy since we both ended up in the same dorm freshman year at FAMU, and she quickly became my best friend again.

Stanton was also segregated into cliques. The jocks (like there were that many at a college prep school for nerds). The richer White kids. The middle-class White kids. The stoners. The nerdiest of nerds. The Black kids. The alternative music kids. I noticed there was one Black boy who only hung out with the White kids. I decided to sit with the Black kids since I didn't know where else to go. I ended up being accepted there and started learning what it meant to be a part of Black culture. It was during those lunches there that I learned how to play Spades and Tonk, both popular card games in Black culture. I became particularly close to Vanessa Chrispin. We'd talk regularly on the phone, usually with me complaining about my controlling mother.

Stanton was filled with amazing teachers. As I mentioned Mr. P and Mr. Rushing were our outstanding AP American & European History teachers, respectively. Junior year I had Ms. Hawley (everyone called her Momma Meg) for English. She was such a great teacher for me, especially since English wasn't my strongest subject (I completely flunked English in eighth grade at Stanton). She made such an impression on me and helped with my exceptionally low self-esteem over those last two years at Stanton. When I reconnected with her on Facebook later in my life, she picked up where she left off, and I have continued and will be eternally grateful for her encouragement and support.

When I took AP Calculus in my senior year, we all had a new teacher, Ms. Marigene Broward. On the first day of class, Ms. Broward told us she had not done Calculus in a long time, but she had taken it over the summer at the community college in preparation and thought she could do a good job teaching us. Her patience and diligence with me are why my grades went from a D in the first quarter to a C in the second quarter, to a B in the third quarter, and an A in the fourth quarter of the year. My father was proud of me, which meant a lot since he didn't talk with me much. I was happy to reconnect with Ms. Broward on Facebook years later because she was one of the people in my life who demonstrated that she believed in my potential and was able to bring it out of me.

I also had an amazing AP Chemistry teacher senior year named Mr. Otto Phanstiel. The way he taught chemistry was so original, unique, and memorable! One time, he was doing an experiment to show us the power of sugar in a test tube he had heated up with a Bunson burner when he dropped a peanut M&M into it, and the peanut shot out of the test tube and through the glass in the classroom door. Who could forget a lesson like that! He taught us about moles with a stuffed mole. He taught us how to turn pennies into gold and silver. He used music based on the song "Delta Dawn" to help us remember the formula for delta H. Oh, the memories of a teacher who loved to teach and was great at it! In fact, his teaching style was so good he and the school's drama teacher wrote a musical about chemistry that won a national award!

That concerned foundation of social wealth is what I left home with in June 1992. Having high school teachers who believed in me helped me build my social wealth through mentorship.

Chapter 4

Part II

Social Wealth
- Branching and Networking

When I got to FAMU, Cindy (my friend from seventh grade at Stanton and later Mandarin) was also there on a full scholarship studying biology pre-med and had internships every summer with Abbott Labs. Back then, we used to write letters to communicate with our friends, or we had to budget for long-distance telephone calls. The calls were expensive, so good old pen and paper in an envelope with a US postal stamp was how I kept in touch with my best friend over the summers. I wrote her letters regularly, sharing my difficulties.

When I didn't hear back from her, I saved up enough money for a long-distance phone call. She shared that she had a roommate (another intern from FAMU) named Caroline "Carrie" Jenkins (later Hepburn). She told me that she and Carrie totally vibed from the beginning and knew they were going to be close friends when they walked out of their respective bedrooms one day wearing the exact same outfit. Carrie taught me that **"People come into your life** for a reason, a season, or a lifetime." She was like a sister to me when my own family of origin dynamics became toxic for me as I started to gain independence from my controlling parents.

When I was a freshman in college at FAMU, I met another LGB scholar from California. By the middle of sophomore year, both of his parents died and left him a lot of money from their life insurance policies. As a roommate, I watched him burn through the money quickly. It was a blessing for me to witness how grief shows up in money from such a safe place. It again reemphasized that **"It's less expensive to learn from someone else's lesson than to have to pay the price yourself."** Ironically, after he spent all his money, he ended up being roommates with my future husband. We actually shared a duplex until my first son was born.

One of the things I can't stress enough when it comes to building wealth of all kinds, specifically social and financial, is how important it is who you choose to marry and/or with whom you choose to procreate. I learned this the hard way from my first marriage. My first husband (father of my firstborn) didn't come from a family like mine. His parents weren't college educated and they divorced while he and his sister were still quite young. When I met him during my freshman year at FAMU while volunteering for the campus SAFE team, he was living in the worst dorms on campus. That should have been my first red flag, but for whatever reason, I knew he was supposed to be a part of my life even before I met him. When I saw his name on a piece of paper, I just knew he was going to be my husband.

Shortly after he and I met, I started seeing an old boyfriend named Walter L. Barnes, II. He was only in town to try to find a full-time job since he had already graduated with his Bachelor of Science degree in Chemical Engineering. He asked me out on a date, but since I was still 17, I told him he would have to ask my parents' permission. To my surprise, I got a call from my mother shortly thereafter telling me that Walter had driven to their home in Jacksonville and asked their permission to date me, which they granted.

After we had been dating for about a month, I put the question to Walter that was on everyone's mind: "Where is this relationship going?" He pondered it for a day or so, then asked me to meet his parents. I did, and he gave me one of his mother's rings to wear as a promise ring for a future betrothal. He then moved to Bettendorf, IA, to start work when I started the spring semester of my freshman year.

While I was tied in heart and mind to Walter, I found myself falling in physical love with my future son's father. I succumbed to the lust between us and made out with him one night that spring of 1993. I couldn't stand the guilt of having cheated on Walter and called him the next evening to relay what had happened. He was hurt. He was broken. He asked questions; delicate questions, and I answered them honestly. At the end of it all, he forgave me.

I was torn after that. I didn't continue my physical relationship with my future son's father, but our mental and spiritual connections increased in those SAFE team volunteer (especially late night) hours. When I moved back to Pensacola, FL, for my second internship with Monsanto, Walter planned a trip to visit me. My dorm room wasn't ready, so I was renting a room in a sorority house on UWF campus - no males allowed. He was gravely disappointed when I wouldn't allow him to stay with me.

When we went to dinner at The Olive Garden. The energy between us was off, and I knew it was me. I just could not see myself committing to a man when I had not even been allowed to date until I was 18 and Walter was so far away. I really knew nothing of men and the world. I could not stand the guilt or the internal conflict, and I broke up with him that night.

I spent my sophomore year mostly at the FAMU/FSU Engineering school. I was surrounded by engineering students all day and most of the night. I continued to date mostly engineering students, but the guy from California captured my heart and mind. I was captivated by his stories of Malcolm X and Minister Louis Farrakhan. I found Al Islam appealing, especially since my mother had raised me not to eat pork, dress modestly, and things like that. Things progressed in our relationship to the point where, on Martin Luther King, Jr. weekend in 1994, I spent the entire weekend with him away from my home. There were no cell phones back then, so when I got home Monday evening, I found a series of voice messages from my mother.

I called her back, and she inquired where I had been all weekend. I told her I was with the guy from L.A. She scolded me and told me it was inappropriate for me to be spending the weekend with a man I wasn't married to. I quickly corrected her and told her we were married. As I understood it at the time, over the weekend, we had entered a Mut'ah marriage. In Al Islam, there are two types of marriage: Mut'ah and Nikah. A Mut'ah marriage is temporary, while a Nikah marriage is permanent. My mother informed me that Mut'ah marriages are what Muslim men use to validate infidelity and prostitution. My mother basically told me I was a prostitute. I debated with my parents and with him for months. It got to the point that he said I was spending so much time with him that I was smothering him. He was looking forward to my upcoming summer internship in Pensacola.

I moved to Pensacola with my parents pressuring me for a permanent marriage (basically one recognized by the state of Florida), but I wasn't sure. I went to visit him in Tallahassee Memorial Day weekend of 1994 and totaled my car on the way back to Pensacola (a health wealth issue to be revealed later). My parents were so distraught that they didn't want me to see him at all. Over the summer, he and I stayed connected with him planning to visit me in Pensacola on the last weekend of July. His mother was a flight attendant with American Airlines, so he could get free flights a lot of the time, but something went wrong that weekend and he ended up flying out to see me the following one, which happened to be my fertile time.

When I got pregnant and moved in with him, he was living in an area of Tallahassee that wasn't the best. In fact, the local drug dealer who lived in the duplex next to us gave us a used twin mattress as a wedding gift since we were sleeping on a twin mattress pad on the floor at that time. On the other side of the duplex we were living in, a welfare mom of three would sit out in the grassless dirt front yard and watch the other residents walk up and down the street while her children did nothing but watch television and get into trouble. My ex-husband called them "porch monkeys," which was a derogatory term for welfare moms who did nothing. Most nights, the neighborhood homeless drunk Mr. J would stop by knocking on doors asking for money. My husband at the time would give him something to eat or a few dollars. Whenever we gave him money, we knew he was just going to go out and buy more alcohol, but we had a heart for the man because he seemed to be mentally ill.

The duplex was filled with German roaches, not the big Florida palmetto bugs. These were the small, nasty, clearly this household has a hygiene problem, kind of little roaches. I've been permanently traumatized by the little eggs they would lay in the lips of the plastic cups we had, which is why I prefer to this day to drink out of a glass. I learned a lot about roaches because I spent

119

a summer researching the pesticides Monsanto was planning to include in their carpet fiber coating. That was my last internship at the Pensacola plant.

The lines in the marriage part that say, "until death do us part" should read, "**until DEBT do us part**," because when I married him, I didn't realize how much financial liability came with that marriage certificate. My husband and I weren't equally yoked when it came to social or financial intelligence.

On our first anniversary, I wanted us to celebrate using the traditional marriage gifts associated with each wedding anniversary, so I bought him a card that said the first anniversary is Paper, and it went on with random things celebrating anniversaries over the years. On the inside, it said, "I don't really know if all of these are right, but I know the first anniversary is Paper. Happy First Anniversary!"

He gave me an $800 Movado watch he'd bought with my credit card! That was his version of (Time/Modern) a first anniversary marriage gift. We argued about it for days, but I made him take it back. Another red flag that we weren't compatible with social or financial wealth. Our financial incompatibility became painfully clear to me one day in the spring of 1996.

I was getting ready for my semiannual dinner with Joe Wiley, my corporate contact from Monsanto and other engineering scholars. Uncle Joe (as I called him) was at a high level in a Fortune 500 company, and I was using that network connection to further my career. My husband was getting ready for work at McDonald's on the night shift. As I looked at the two of us in the mirror of our bathroom, I had an epiphany. We weren't going in the same direction.

I returned home that night seriously thinking about my social wealth. What was I doing married to a McDonald's employee who couldn't even keep his grades up to study architecture? When I started work at the Monsanto St. Louis Carondelet plant over that summer, I met another chemical engineering intern who was a Black male. He was six-five, handsome, and smart as a whip. He was from St. Louis and was participating in the Inroads program through Texas A&M University.

He didn't say much but was often in my cubicle talking with the other intern and the young engineer I shared space with. When I looked at him each day in my cubicle and then looked at my husband when I went home to the trailer at night, I just didn't see the fit with my husband in the long run.

However, when I found out I was going to be interning in St. Louis, MO, my husband exercised his social wealth and found a place for us to live. We'd be sharing a mobile home with his stepsister behind his step-grandmother's house. It would help us all out if we rented a room in the trailer for the summer. When I agreed to the arrangement, I had no idea what neighborhood we'd be living in. All I knew was the address was in Brooklyn, Illinois.

We arrived at Big Momma's house (his step-grandmother) in the middle of the night after driving our U-Haul cross-country from Tallahassee. As we got closer, I noticed the pornography stores and strip clubs that were on the way. I was uncomfortable but kept going. I knew that **"You are the average of the five people you spend the most time with,"** and I was conscious that the neighborhood we lived in would affect that. I forged on. I was the breadwinner at the time, and my husband was refusing to get a job. I needed a job to pay our bills, so I did the best I could to adapt. When I pressured my husband to get a job, he said I made enough money to take care of us, and he was tired from watching our toddler all day. We tried marriage counseling a few times to no

121

avail. I worked hard that summer and came home one day (August 2, 1996) to a Dear John letter.

"Dear Njeri, I have gone to file for divorce. This is a relationship I no longer want to be in. Don't bother coming to California, as that will only make things worse. I will call in a few days to make arrangements for Shorty."

I was devastated that my child had been taken from me (across state lines) by my husband! I immediately called my parents, and they told me to go to the police. I went to the Brooklyn police station, and they took a statement, but because there was no divorce in progress, there wasn't a thing they could do. Eventually, my husband's father and stepmother flew in with my husband to try to straighten things out. They convinced him to stay and help me drive back to Tallahassee, although my child was in Los Angeles.

When we returned to our duplex, my husband immediately cleared out all his belongings and left. I was to start school again within a week, and there was no discussion about when he was bringing our child back to Florida. My parents told me to see an attorney, so I scraped up $75 for a consultation with a divorce lawyer. I told him my situation and that both my husband and I were living in Tallahassee while our child was in LA with my husband's family. The attorney said that since there was no divorce in progress, I should go get my child.

I then called my husband's stepmother to get the address but didn't disclose my plan to retrieve my son. I booked a roundtrip ticket to Los Angeles with just enough time on the ground to collect my child and return home. I wasn't prepared for what would happen.

When I arrived at their apartment complex, my husband's stepmother refused to allow me access past the front gate. I called the police to tell them I was there to regain custody of my child.

While they were on their way, my husband's father pulled his car into the driveway to the apartment complex gate and parked. He then took my son and placed him on the front seat of the car with no car seat or protection. When I tried to open the passenger door to get my son, he locked the door. I tried to reach over my husband's father to get him, but he took his size 14 foot and kicked me in my chest to the ground, then closed and locked the driver's side door. I then ran to stand behind the car to prevent him from driving off before the police came, but his wife came out and dragged me from behind the car so they could leave.

I went to the nearest police station to file a report, but nothing came of it. While I was waiting outside the police station, a security guard saw me and asked if I needed help. I told him of my situation and that I needed a place to go for several hours while I waited for my return flight to Florida. He offered to take me to his home, and I graciously agreed. His wife made us some Ramen noodles, and I was grateful for their hospitality. A stranger saw a young woman in need of support and offered to help. That was a spark of good social wealth in a horrible moment.

I returned to Florida and sought a divorce attorney. It was over $750 for her just to file the paperwork for divorce and custody after she met with me. Then she called me and said, "I met your husband at the courthouse. Just as I was about to file your papers, he had already filed his. They wouldn't serve me with all your papers because, apparently, he has filed a domestic violence injunction against you."

I was shocked! Domestic violence? We had never exchanged more than words with each other. How could he claim domestic violence? My attorney assured me that she could handle the case, but it was going to cost me more than I had. I turned to my parents and asked for assistance, especially since they had pressured me into marrying him in the first place. They denied me any financial assistance.

Thankfully, because I was on welfare, I qualified for non-profit legal services. The attorney assigned to my case was Gordon Cherr. When he presented the papers to me, I was shocked. My soon-to-be ex-husband had claimed that I would kill him. Ultimately, I was awarded full custody with minimal child support at $250 per month. I also later learned that he filed a domestic violence claim to get custody of our son. He lied and said I would kill him when the truth was he had read my diary the night before he left and read that I had planned to leave him when we got back to Tallahassee. My exact words were, "Leaving him will be like killing him in his sleep... he won't even realize what's happened until it's over." He decided to do to me what he had read I planned to do to him.

That divorce was my introduction to the legal system in this country, and boy, did I learn a lot. For example, Iowa does not play when it comes to child support. During the process and time of fighting to get my son back while I lived in Muscatine in 2007, the court in Iowa updated the child support amount and filed a claim on my ex-husband's tax return. I was elated when, years later, he and his new wife's tax return was deposited in me and my current husband's account for back child support. Hats off to Iowa!

We went through another custody battle after my health wealth was depleted in February 2007. In an emergency situation, I sent our son to live with him. During the time I had to myself, I reached out to Joe Wiley about Jackie Gaul, who I had heard glowing reports about at both the Luling and Muscatine plants. She had climbed the corporate ladder at Monsanto and retired as the VP of ESH for the company. I told Joe I wanted to meet her, and he set it up. I drove down from Muscatine to St. Louis to meet her for dinner. Within 10 minutes of that conversation, she invited me to join her and her family for Easter in Perth, Scotland.

During that trip she dropped A LOT of knowledge for me on how to navigate the corporate world in America, especially within Monsanto. During one of our talks, I asked her if she grew up in Louisiana since she was Creole. Her reply has always stuck with me: "I grew up in Louisiana. I grew up in Muscatine. I grew up in St. Louis." What I got from that is **never stop growing. Everywhere you live, there is an opportunity to grow.** I asked her if she learned any Creole French from her parents. She told me they only spoke it when they wanted their privacy.

While with her during that week in Scotland, I soaked up a lot of her wisdom and had an epiphany while I observed her daughter (a Black woman) and her Scottish husband (a White man) as they tended to their one-year-old daughter. I realized that I DID want to be married again and DID want to have another child.

That epiphany, the "Her Ladyship" mug I purchased on my trip, and the powerful advice and suggestions I received while visiting Scotland stunted my progress up the corporate American ladder at Monsanto. My White male counterparts were put off by my pulling strings to gain knowledge and social wealth, implementing what I learned and going after what I wanted. Their retaliation was to use one of the few Black male engineers I had become close to at the Muscatine plant to deliver their warning. I duly noted it and continued my quest to fulfill my purpose.

125

Chapter 4

Part III

Social Wealth:
How I Met My Husband

Picture it, New Orleans, The year 2000.

It's the day after Thanksgiving, and I'm leaving the Bayou Classic at the Superdome with my girlfriend Melva Langston (now Martin). I had met her through the Black male chemical engineer who went to college with her at Texas A&M, and I had met him as an intern in St. Louis. As I'm walking down the street, I see a guy who looks so familiar walking with an older man.

"I know that guy. I know that guy. I know that guy," I say to myself as I pass him on the street.

"Jerome Robicheaux!" I exclaimed aloud and turned around.

"Njeri Gichia!" he responded as he turned to face me.

It was, in fact, my old friend from FAMU, Jerome Robicheaux.

We had originally met as Life Gets Better scholars at FAMU in Tallahassee in the fall of 1992. We had both been engineering students (him for electrical and me for chemical) when we met in the grand ballroom at an orientation session for LGB scholars.

There had been an initial attraction, but as a freshman, I was focused elsewhere.

When we reconnected as fully formed adults with children, we were both in a survival space. As anyone who has ever been a single parent will tell you, there is a sort of survival frequency you live on as a single parent.

He had relocated back to his hometown, New Orleans, from Ohio (where his wife and daughters' mother was from) and was going through a divorce. Our first-born children were just a few months apart, so it made sense for us to arrange play dates.

My social life at the time consisted of nights out on the town drinking with my coworkers, whose motto was, "The liver is evil, so it must be punished!" Having another parent to hang with was a good alternative. After several months of hanging out both with and without our kids, Jerome's birthday rolled around, and he hosted a barbeque at his family home and introduced me to them. As soon as I walked into the kitchen, I made myself useful and felt like family. His mother, Ms. Annette Robicheaux, embraced me as if I was her own daughter. It wasn't until later that I learned it was because she thought Jerome and I were dating. Then the unthinkable happened.

It was Tuesday, September 11, 2001. I was at work finishing a review of the chemical processes I was responsible for as I prepared to head to the airport for a business trip. That is when our process trainer told me I wasn't going anywhere. A plane had just flown into one of the towers of the World Trade Center, and all airports were closed. I literally watched as the second plane hit the second tower, and both buildings collapsed. At the time, my best friend Cindy was living with her boyfriend, who worked at the Pentagon. It took forever, but eventually, I spoke with her, and she assured me they were all fine.

A few days later, Jerome and I went out for a cocktail. We sat there together at the bar, and he put the question to me, *There's no excuse for my or my parents' behavior,* "Where is this relationship going?"

"What do you mean?" I replied.

"Well, we have been dating for over a year," Jerome said.

"Dating?!" I exclaimed. "Aren't you still married?"

"Well, no, the divorce isn't final, but..." he said.

"But what?" I said. "I don't date married men."

And that was that. Well, not exactly. You see, a few months later, my maternal grandmother died, and Jerome was my first call. When I told him, he let me know he would be over to my townhouse as quickly as he could. I took a shower, put on my pajamas and sleep bonnet, and answered the door when he arrived. Imagine my surprise when I opened the door, and there he stood with RaeLynn Song. I had met her before at one of Jerome's business-friendly get-togethers but didn't think much about the two of them together.

I invited them in, and they proceeded to comfort me in my grief. It was a welcome but awkward visit. A few days later, I called Jerome to discuss the exchange. I explained to him that I didn't date married men, but that didn't mean I would never date him, just not if he was legally married. He explained that he had already grown close to RaeLynn and didn't want to hurt her feelings. I told him I completely understood and would support their relationship.

Over the next several years, he repeatedly tried to introduce me to his best friend. "Your birthdays are two days apart. He is a mechanical engineer and lives in Orlando." Every time his best friend Darryl Broussard came to New Orleans, Jerome would try to introduce us, but either I would leave before Darryl arrived, or he would leave before I arrived.

Jerome and I stayed in regular contact while he courted RaeLynn. I shared with him what I had been reading about the "in love" chemicals that the brain produces and how it takes 12 to 18 months for them to decrease back to normal. I told him how I had learned that a man shows the woman he's courting how serious the relationship is getting by buying her jewelry, working his way down the arms to the ring finger by first buying her earrings, then a necklace, then a bracelet, and finally an engagement ring. He listened to my advice as he courted RaeLynn and continued to try to introduce me to Darryl.

After a couple of years, Jerome proposed to RaeLynn, and she accepted. After I heard her say, "Our kids," referring to Jerome's three girls (who are like nieces to me), I knew they would be a great married couple. I even made a point to corner RaeLynn in the bathroom one night and let her know I wasn't a threat to their relationship and fully supported their marriage.

The wedding was going to be on October 9, 2004, in Auckland, New Zealand which is where most of RaeLynn's family lives. Since it was her first wedding, about 30 of us decided to fly to New Zealand for the wedding. Darryl was now engaged and would be Jerome's best man.

Those of us arriving congregated at RaeLynn's parents' house. A girlfriend and I were sitting at the dining room table when Jerome announced that his best man and his fiancée had just landed and were on their way there.

I thought to myself, *let's see this guy Jerome's been trying to introduce me to for so many years.* When Darryl walked in, all I could do was look away to hide the smile on my face and think, *why does he have to be engaged?!* He was gorgeous!

That evening, a group of us went out to dinner late and Darryl's fiancée didn't join us. We were all talking and laughing and having a good time. I could feel a chemistry between Darryl and me, but I tried to ignore it.

The next morning, I went to Jerome's hotel room down the hall from mine to help him with his daughters. Darryl showed up. He and his fiancée were staying at a hotel across the street, and their room didn't have a phone book. He wanted to borrow Jerome's phone book to look something up. They searched the room, and I even helped them look for quite a while, but we could not find one in the room, so I offered Darryl to use the one in my room.

We walked to my hotel room, having a cordial conversation the whole time. I gave him my phone book, and he looked up whatever he needed as we continued our conversation. Time passed, and we continued talking with the chemistry between us undeniable. I stood in the corner of the room to "avoid the appearance of evil," fully aware that he was engaged and, during the conversation, slipped in that I had grown up Episcopalian. I told him that we as Episcopalians, take a vow as guests at the ceremony to support the marriage. I told him to invite me to his wedding. He laughed it off. At some point during the conversation, he lay back on my bed and dare I say, he looked quite attractive. He had that Freddie Jackson, Luther Vandross, Marvin Gaye lean you would see on their CD covers. Then he looked me dead in my eyes and asked me the strangest question, "Would you have another child?"

I grew dizzy. My future flashed before my eyes. Before I could say, "No," God said, "Yes!" for me. I was shocked when I heard myself say, "Yes!" Up until then, my mind had been decidedly against having more children. I had even made an agreement with my firstborn when he was six that if he didn't make me a Cucu (which is Kikuyu for grandmother) before I was 50, I would be available to help him raise his children, but the idea was that I would have my forties to myself. This encounter with Darryl

131

weirdly happened before the trip to Scotland when I realized that my YES response to him was truer than I knew at the time. It may have taken 10 years, but I believe he got me pregnant with our son Matthew the moment he asked the question, leaning on a bed in my hotel room having a casual conversation. No wonder the only song that captures the tone of my relationship with Darryl is "Un-Thinkable" by Alicia Keyes.

I had to act quickly to get rid of him after that question. Clove cigarettes (a bad habit I picked up from the guy I had been dating off and on in New Orleans since I moved to Louisiana)! I decided to tell him I was going outside to smoke a clove cigarette and invited him to join me to continue the conversation. I figured if he were okay with me smoking clove cigarettes, then he could not be the one. When he declined and said he needed to get back to his room, I went outside to smoke and watched him cross the street. *What just happened?* I thought to myself.

The next day I spent with Jerome's oldest sister touring Auckland and visiting the city museum. There was an exhibit showing the migration from Asia to New Zealand. She asked a question that has stuck with me ever since, "What made them decide to leave one island for another?" I have long since pondered that question as I continue with my own life. The next evening there was the bachelor/bachelorette party at a local Auckland club. I arrived earlier with my girlfriend and had a couple of drinks. When Jerome and RaeLynn walked in with Darryl behind them and no fiancée in sight, I was intrigued. The group proceeded to party and had a good time listening to some US music mixed in by the DJ. Then, the unthinkable happened.

The mood was set. The strings were playing. And Juvenile's "Back That Thang Up" started playing. I looked over at my girlfriend after I saw the smile on Darryl's face and said to her, "Let's see how serious he is about that fiancée." Long story short, I went to dance with him, and did, in fact, back that thang up. After a while, Jerome's colleague showed up, and I left Darryl on the dance floor since I would be sharing a room with Jerome's colleague for the rest of the weekend.

That Saturday at the reception, Jerome's colleague and I were seated together at the same table as Darryl's fiancée. Darryl was seated at the head table with the bridal party. Now, why is this important? Well, when the dance part of the reception came up, there was a soul train line, so, I decided to participate since I do love to dance. Jerome's colleague declined. I inched my way up the line alone, and when I got to the head of my line, Darryl got up from the head table, walked past the table where his fiancée was seated and skipped everyone on the other side of the line to go down the middle with me! I must admit I had a good time meeting and testing the waters with Darryl at the wedding. I didn't think about him again until June 2007 when I was showing my coworkers pictures of my trip to New Zealand and came across the picture of us dancing down the Soul Train line together.

I went back to New Orleans after the wedding and dropped my plans to travel to two new US states each year in exchange for visiting a new country every year. At the time, I was reading Dan Brown's *The Da Vinci Code* and had learned that he had other books out, including *Angels & Demons,* set in Italy. My friend Kim Sanders (now Leniar) and I agreed to go to Italy together and read the book while we were there. I really wanted to see the sculpture of St. Theresa's Ecstasy since I had a vision of seeing it years earlier during my dual enrollment humanities class in high school at Stanton. Shortly after I returned from New Zealand,

Kim announced that she was engaged and wouldn't be able to take the trip with me.

I wanted to fully enjoy a whole school year without my son, so I decided to travel anyway. I asked the guy I had been dating whether he wanted to go to Paris or Italy. He said Paris. I asked if he wanted to go for Mardi Gras or Easter. He said Easter. With that, I booked my flight to Rome and called him to coordinate.

He then dropped the bomb on me. "I am not going to Paris with you!" I was offended, appalled, yet motivated. Even though I had studied French for four years and would have preferred my first international trip alone be to a place where I would at least be able to communicate with the locals, something in me told me to keep the reservation to Italy, read *Angels and Demons*, and let God do the rest.

I booked my hotel room in Rome on the way to the airport, along with a train ride to and from Florence to see Michelangelo's David. I felt like I was on a trip led by God as I read the book. When I got back to Rome from Florence that Thursday, I searched for the church featuring the St. Theresa's Ecstasy sculpture, according to the book. As I crossed Piazza Bernini, I just knew God wanted me to find something. I walked up the stairs to the church and noticed a father and daughter together. Was I here to learn to heal from my father's emotional abandonment? I tried the door of the church but found it locked. I looked out over the Piazza and noticed three men walking in the direction of the church. I heard God tell me to wait, so I did. I watched them walk across the Piazza and up the stairs to the door I knew was already locked. Not knowing what language they spoke, I just shook my head and pointed up the stairs to the main door. Then I heard God tell me to go up the stairs as well and try the main door. I did, found it locked, and heard from behind me, "Looks like it's closed."

I turned around and saw the tall one who had spoken to me and responded with, "Well, that sucks." He then said, "We're about to go to the Spanish Steps to watch the sun go down. Do you want to come?"

I heard God say for me, "Yes!"

Then there I was, walking down the streets of Rome with three strange men. Along the walk, they introduced themselves. One was from Australia. One was from Canada. And the tall one was from Norway named Espen. He shared that he was from a small town called Tønsberg, and he had left there at the beginning of the year since he was going through a divorce. He had found his Vietnamese wife coming out of a hotel room with one of his good friends. He was traveling south until he ran out of money.

When we arrived at the Spanish Steps, the four of us were just in time to watch the sun go down. While we were watching it, Espen and I noticed a Black couple who shared a toddler arguing. The police got involved.

I looked at them and said, "I know what that's like."

Espen replied, "I am sure you do."

The look of depression on his face had me thinking, *he needs to laugh.* I decided to tell him a story about a visit to my third sister's home. She had just had twins, and my other two sisters and I went to visit her to help with the babies. When I came into the kitchen, I was looking for a place to sit and have my breakfast, but there was this giant cardboard box on the table. I asked my sister if it was heavy so I could move it without injuring myself, and she said, "No. It's a box full of straws." I was perplexed. She then said, "My husband is a compulsive shopper. He saw a deal on a box full of straws and couldn't resist."

She and I both laughed as I easily moved the box from the table to one of the empty chairs. My third sister told that story three times as each of my other sisters entered the kitchen. At the end of it all four of us were laughing as we ate breakfast. Then one sister asked, "So what are you going to do with all those straws?"

My host sister replied, as she pulled out a bundle of the straws, "I don't know. Maybe we'll give them away as parting gifts. Thank you for coming! I hope your visit didn't suck!" We all burst into laughter, and as I told Espen, he broke into laughter too.

At that point, the sun had set and the three of them were heading back to the youth hostel where they were staying. When we got to the corner, the other two spoke to Espen who then said to me, "They're tired and going back to the youth hostel, but I think I'm going to stay with you." He asked me to join him for dinner, to which I agreed but told him I had to stop at an internet café first to make my daily blog post so my mother wouldn't lose it thinking I had been kidnapped, murdered, or something else.

I loved that trip so much that I decided to share it with others on my blog. Here's a taste of what I shared:

Tuesday, February 8, 2005, 3:18 PM

So, what happened yesterday? Went to the Colosseum...big, old, and ridiculously priced to get inside. Pics from outside were good enough for me. I then went off in search of the "Fire" church referenced in Angels & Demons to no avail. I will have to look into that when I get back to Rome...I feel a real connection to that Saint ;-) After I gave up looking for it, I took a trip to the Pantheon, Piazza Navona (Water), and Trevi fountain. They are all impressive in pictures, but when you see them in person, it's like, "Geez Louise!" This is some serious art! It's truly overwhelming after a while.

Friday, February 11, 2005, 3:56 PM

It's hard to believe it's Friday already & I am returning home to-morrow. I feel like I have lived through some sort of metamorphosis. I will be returning tomorrow with so many questions answered...and more questions now than before I left in the first place! Such is life.

I spent the rest of the evening and well into the night with the Norwegian. I felt like a teenager having to wake up the hotel staff to get in at 2:30 in the morning. The guard scowled at me like I was a naughty girl for being out so late. Who would have thought love could find me so soon and be so ironic.

Well, I am still searching for Santa Maria Della Vittoria...it's my last attempt before I return tomorrow. Otherwise, I will talk with you all tomorrow when I am back on US soil.

Ciao!

When I returned to Louisiana from Italy, my ideas about human connection (especially sexually) changed forever. You see, that morning I had arrived back in Rome from Florence, I awakened to my cycle starting five days early, so I had to find a pharmacy to get protection. I didn't know why my cycle had started so early until Espen kissed me that night, dropped me off at my hotel, and gave me his contact information that I realized God had wanted me to experience emotional intimacy without sex. You see, Espen and I connected spiritually in spite of the physical chemistry between us. We were kindred spirits. I guess that's why he continued to encourage me to read *The Celestine Prophecy* after we both went home. We experienced true intimacy: Into Me See.

I decided to move on from Louisiana once I realized the one who decided not to go to Paris with me was being a jackass, not just to me but to everyone around him he considered equal to or beneath him. I realized that all along, it wasn't me. IT WAS HIM! I didn't think enough of myself to require more of a man. When I came back from St. Louis for the Monsanto MESH conference in May 2005, I immediately requested a transfer to another facility. I knew it was the only way I was going to permanently break off that toxic relationship.

I kept in touch with Espen and agreed to visit him in Norway for a week that August. I had always wanted to see the Aurora Borealis, and that would be a good time to go. Was he "the one" or just a "kindred spirit" sent to teach me a lesson? I decided to investigate more after eventually reading *The Celestine Prophecy*. Before I booked my flight to Norway, I called my parents. My mother answered the phone on speaker.

I told her I had finally decided to visit the Norwegian in Norway. She asked why I didn't have him come to New Orleans since he had already expressed an interest in visiting. I told her I thought it wiser to observe him in his natural environment to get a better feel for him. We talked a bit longer, and eventually, I asked her what she thought about my plans to visit. "Well, your daddy's been listening, and he thinks you should follow your heart." I was taken aback that my father had been listening and that he approved!

I took the trip and, alas, came home with the answer; he was a kindred spirit meant to be in my life for a season. That became abundantly clear after Hurricane Katrina hit New Orleans, and he didn't call to check on me.

When the summer of 2006 came, I was ready for my move back to Muscatine, IA. I would focus on my career and if a relationship developed, so be it. I was quickly acquainted with a young Brazilian accountant from Bahia who introduced me to Match.com. I tried it with my location being Muscatine, IA, but didn't make any matches. I expanded my search area to include the Quad Cities. I also stated that I was willing to relocate. I dated a few people, but after I went to Scotland in April 2007, I came back with a clearer vision of what I wanted romantically and knew how critical my decision would be for my social wealth. I wanted to be married again, and I wanted to have another child.

After my New Orleans JazzFest trip in May 2007, I had my final contact with the former coworker/lover. I came back to Iowa from that trip and wrote down a prayer to God to send me a man who would be unlike my former lover but committed to me and only me, as I had learned watching my family's marriages and through reading the Bible, and as I had witnessed through the Episcopal church. I prayed for my purpose to be fulfilled long before I realized marriage is a ministry for me.

That summer on a Friday afternoon, I was showing my coworkers pictures from my trip to New Zealand as they were intrigued by my wanderlust. I came across a picture of me dancing down the Soul Train line with Darryl. All I could think to myself was, *"We had such great chemistry...why did he have to be engaged?"*

The next day I got a call at home from Jerome to catch up. He, RaeLynn, and the rest of their family had settled in Sarasota, FL after his family home was flooded by Hurricane Katrina. He mentioned that Darryl had been asking about me.

"Isn't he married?" I inquired.

Jerome mumbled something about a divorce and emphasized that his friend wanted to get in touch with me. I couldn't for the life of me think of why but when Jerome asked if he could give Darryl my cell phone number, I told him to give him my work email address instead. The following is the exchange between us via email that Monday.

From: Broussard, Darryl A.
Sent: Monday, June 18, 2007, 7:03 AM
Njeri,

I thought I would drop you a line and see how you have been. Hopefully, you remember me by name. Anyway, I guess it will have been about three years since Jerome's wedding when I first met you. Jerome told me you are working at Monsanto...in Iowa? How have you been?

I have been good. Still living in sunny Orlando, FL...not too far from Jerome and family. If you remember, I was engaged at the time we met. I got married and then divorced. No kids and thank God things were amicable. Anyway, I thought about you and was wondering what you were up to nowadays. What is new with you?

Hope to hear from you sometime.

Take care,

Darryl Broussard

From: GICHIA, NJERI A
Sent: Monday, June 18, 2007, 10:13 AM

Darryl,

Of course, I remember you! I am doing well, living in Muscatine, IA. I guess I have been here for going on a year. There's not much going on in my life as of late, just focused on my career and planning my next move.

Where in Orlando do you live? Is your family from that area? My parents moved from there just after Jerome's wedding, so I am fairly familiar with the area. I'll actually be seeing Jerome and RaeLynn in Tampa in August. It's funny that when Jerome called me, I had just been looking at the pictures from the wedding the day before! You'd crossed my mind as well.........

It's good to hear that you had an amicable divorce and didn't have children involved. Hopefully, we'll get a chance to chat in the near future and you can tell me more.

Warm Regards,

Njeri

The emails back in forth went on for hours, the last one on June 18th, Darryl said he would call me later. When I got home that evening, I was nervous. Was he really going to call? What does he want?

When he did call, I used what I had learned from reading *Why Men Love Bitches* and let it go to voicemail. I purposely waited 20 minutes to call him back. I centered myself before I dialed. When he answered, the conversation was effortless, much like it had been when we first met.

We ended up talking more frequently on the phone on nights and weekends as well as communicating via email while at work. After a month or so he asked me if I came to Florida often to visit Jerome and RaeLynn. He said he'd like to see me in person again. I told him that my sisters and I had our sisters' weekend scheduled in Tampa in early August. I was planning to meet up with Jerome and RaeLynn there the night before for dinner and dancing. He asked if he could invite himself along since he hadn't seen the couple in a while. I agreed.

When I flew to Tampa, I arrived just in time to join the group for dinner. We were all laughing and having a great time. We then went to a club called Kismet. While there, Darryl and I were getting closer. At some point, something in me thought, *when is he going to kiss me?* Eventually, he did, and both RaeLynn and Jerome were thrilled. RaeLynn then disclosed that when Jerome took a picture of the two of us dancing down the Soul Train line at their wedding reception, she told him, "We should be trying to get those two together!" Apparently, not many of Darryl's friends liked his second wife, who he was engaged to when we met.

Previously, he had asked me where I was staying since my sisters weren't arriving in Tampa until Saturday afternoon. I told him I was staying at my girlfriend's place nearby. He asked if he could stay with me, and I said, "Uh, I don't think that's a good idea." So, when we left the club and he dropped me off at my girlfriend's place, he kissed me and said, "You're really going to make me stay at a hotel?"

"Yes," I flatly responded.

He left and I went inside and talked with my girlfriend's husband, a budding pastor. He applauded me for not giving in to sex too early in the relationship as I was sticking with the 90-day rule where the couple does not become sexually intimate and there is an agreement to exclusivity.

When I woke the next morning Darryl had already asked me out for breakfast and for our first official date, which was going to the gun range. It was then that I told him I was a Republican, and he was shocked. I told him I believed in smaller government and that the economy was better off with capitalism in play because the private sector was more efficient than the government. That's led to lots of interesting conversations between us over the years, as he is a diehard Democrat.

At any rate, the time came for me to check into the hotel room my sisters and I were sharing for the weekend, and he brought my things to the room for me. We kissed. He asked how long it was going to be before my sisters arrived. I told him it was going to be soon and (as I was feeling more excited) it was probably time for him to go. Darryl walked me down to the lobby just as my sisters were arriving. From a distance, they watched him kiss me good-bye with their elder sisters' watchful eyes. Darryl called later to tell me he wanted to plan a trip to visit me in Muscatine around our birthdays in mid-October. I agreed and told him that the fall foliage should be in full bloom at that time, so the town would be beautiful.

As we continued to communicate, I was resistant to the idea of falling in love with him. He had been married and divorced twice and lived with a woman with three children for a while. Those were significant concerns for me. One night in late August, I could not sleep and decided to walk from my condo to the town riverfront on the Mississippi to watch the sun rise. Once I got there, I did something unusual and called my mother. I told her about Darryl and how we had been communicating increasingly. I told her I didn't want to fall in love with him too quickly the way I did with the Norwegian to which she replied, "I think you're already in love with him."

She advised me to date him through four seasons, figuratively and literally. See him in every type of situation possible. That would allow me time to see if our VALUES matched and hopefully for the in-love chemicals to die down. We continued communicating, and at some point, in early September 2007, we started talking about wealth. I shared with him that I had read *The Millionaire Next Door,* and one of my goals was to be a millionaire by the time I was 50. He was impressed and asked to know more. I told him that I had created a spreadsheet to calculate my accumulator of wealth score so I could keep track of how I was doing. I offered to send it to him, and he accepted. The following was our communication:

From: *GICHIA, NJERI A*

D,

I have attached the wealth test I mentioned yesterday. It's set up to link to other files I have saved for automatic updates, so you'll need to enter your own information.

<<wealth.xls>>

Later,

Njeri

From: *Broussard, Darryl A*

Well, I have some work to do! The wealth test definitely reminds me to get cracking with some more investing and taking care of some old debts. I don't think I am doing bad at all, but plenty can be done to put my money in the right places, instead of foolish spending...got to look to the future! I'll finish adding to it and let you see how things look.

So, is this your "dating application" for potentials??? When submitted for processing, how long before one gets the OK to date you? Does dating come with a probation period...periodic reviews... bonuses for good performance...exclusive benefits...penalties for wastefulness and overindulgence...???

I hope all went well today. Call me when you get a chance after you get on the road.

D

I was on my way to St. Louis for a business trip when I called him after that exchange. I said something to him about me not dating anyone, and he said to me, "I'm dating you!"

I responded with, "Oh well, if that is the case then I'm going to need to see all three of your credit reports and your FICO scores."

"What?!" he exclaimed.

144

"Yeah, I mean, there's no point in us dating if our FICO scores don't match," I flatly replied.

He was taken aback. That Sunday, he met Jerome in Tampa for a Saints football game. He had told Jerome what I said, and Jerome laughed and said, "Yeah, that sounds like Njeri!"

The next day, Darryl called me and said, "I'll show you mine if you show me yours."

I had no problem with that, so we got **financially naked**. Once he saw my FICO scores and all the wealth I had accumulated to that point where we'd both been working the same number of years as engineers and I had been a single parent, he immediately turned his finances over to me.

A couple of weeks later, I got a call from one of my sisters telling me my oldest nephew had been having suicidal thoughts and had been Baker Acted. I decided it was time to be transparent with Darryl about my health wealth since we were moving forward. I shared I had been suffering from anxiety and depression for years and about a difficult situation with my son earlier that year. He was understanding and accepting. I was relieved. He was supportive of my prayers for my nephew after I told him what was going on with him and that depression runs in my family. He didn't seem to be put off. I asked him how he felt about me knowing all of this, and he said, "When I get to Iowa, I'm going to tell you how I feel about you."

He came to Muscatine in October 2007, and he was only the third man I had dated that I introduced to my son. He was the first I allowed to sleep in my home with my son's knowledge, but I had a guest room. My oldest son's eyes were blue when he was born. Everyone told me they would change as he got older. They do change to grey, and when he is incredibly angry, they turn Incredible Hulk GREEN! Well, that's what color his eyes were

145

when he entered the living room and saw Darryl sitting next to me on the couch. He later confessed that he was jealous because he feared Darryl had "taken his spot!"

At one point during the visit, Darryl and I were alone in the rose garden in Weed Park. While there, I asked Darryl how he felt about me, and he said, "How do I feel about you? I'm in love with you!"

The butterfly feeling in my stomach was so strong I felt like I was going to throw up. Although Isaiah was put off by Darryl at first, he and Darryl had a good time during the visit. We ALL did! And the best part was after Darryl left my nephew called me on my birthday to wish me happy birthday. He had been discharged on his 20th birthday (which was five days before mine) and put on Lexapro to manage his depression. He was excited because he was starting a new job at a movie theater the following week. I shared my news about Darryl and told my nephew I couldn't wait for them to meet. Then he did something we don't often do in our family. He said, "I love you, Aunt Njeri!" I told him I loved him too, not knowing it was the last time we'd speak.

When I learned of his death, I was at a local game night in Muscatine with my son. I knew something was wrong when I subsequently got calls from each of my sisters and my mother. When I heard the news, I was shocked and immediately took my son home. I called my Brazilian friend from work and left her a message. I called Darryl and left him a message. He called me back shortly and was incredibly supportive. He asked when the funeral would be, and I told him the following week in Jacksonville. Of course, Isaiah and I were planning to fly down. He offered to drive up and attend the funeral with us. I thought better of it since I knew it was going to be an extremely emotional event, and he'd never met my nephew.

I told him my sister and her husband were hosting a get-to-gether at their house after the funeral, and he could come there to see us if he wanted to. He said he would. I explained that I had only brought two other men home to meet my family in my life and one of them was already my husband. He said he understood. I told him this was a very serious move, and I would understand if he didn't want to come. He said he wanted to be there for me and my family. I wanted to disclose everything so he wasn't caught off guard.

After the service, 40 to 50 friends and family descended on my sister's home. When Darryl called me from outside to confirm it was the right house, I told him I would meet him in the driveway to confirm. We met outside and he asked me how the funeral went. I told him it was surreal. I asked him if he was sure he wanted to walk into that house. He said he was sure. I reminded him that I had only really brought one boyfriend home and that it was considered serious in our family. He reconfirmed that he understood. We stood out there talking like that for about 30 minutes when my sister (the hostess) poked her head out the front door and asked if everything was okay. We assured her it was, and she asked, "So are y'all coming in or not?"

We promptly entered the house, and I started introducing Darryl to various family and friends. We made our way to the kitchen table, where my father and mother were seated together. I introduced him, and he took a seat next to my father. I took a seat on the other side of the table. I was so nervous while he and my father were talking that my cousin's wife leaned over to me and said, "Relax, girl!" I tried to relax, but sure enough, within 15 minutes of them starting to talk, I overheard my father talking about our Kikuyu tribe and the dowry process for marriage. I figured if that didn't scare him off, nothing would!

We continued dating through the winter and into the spring. He traveled to Arizona and California a lot for work, so he would arrange his trips so he could "stop by" Muscatine. I even created a spreadsheet that tracked our visit schedule. He'd already told me he was studying to get his real estate broker's license so he and his father could start their own business. His father was a Wharton MBA and business consultant living in South Florida. Darryl told me that when he'd purchased his first home and saw what the Realtor® got paid he figured he could do it too, so he got his sales associate's license and had been selling real estate on the side for four years. Now, he wanted to level up and own his own real estate brokerage firm. I was impressed, especially after he passed his broker's exam on the second try!

The first week of that December I was scheduled for an environmental business conference in Orlando for a week. We took the opportunity to get together each evening. One night, he told me he wanted to introduce me to his best friend, Socrate Exantus, and his wife, Cassandra. They had just had their first child and brought their baby girl home from the hospital. When we arrived at their sprawling home, I was taken aback at Socrate's high level of energy. Socrate was a midlevel manager at Sprint at the time, and Cassandra was a Realtor® working with a builder. Cassandra introduced herself and said she was tired and going to bed, knowing I would understand because I was a mother. I laughed and wished her great rest. Darryl, Socrate and I talked as Socrate glowed, holding his baby girl.

When I returned for Christmas break a few weeks later, Darryl and I went to dinner with his friend Dwight Sands and his wife Claudell. Darryl was their Realtor® for a home in the same community where he built the house with his second wife.

148

Dwight has been a good resource for investment information for Darryl over the years.

After that week we planned to spend my Christmas break together in Florida and then join my two closest friends and their significant others for New Year's Eve in New York City. One day, while we were walking through the city, we found ourselves on 5th Avenue. Then we just happened to find ourselves in front of Tiffany's®. We decided to go inside and there we found ourselves in the engagement ring section. He asked me what kind of ring I liked. I pointed out a three-stone past, present, and future setting. He asked if my ring had to come from Tiffany's. "Oh no!" I responded, "But it does need to be a total of at least two carats."

The trip to New York was a welcome distraction. My friends really liked Darryl. We were deeply in love, and everyone could see it. That March, we were discussing who should move so our relationship could go to the next level. He suggested I move in with him. My response?

"Have you MET me?" I flatly asked.

"What do you mean?" he asked.

"Why would I move in with you?" I quizzed.

"Well, we love each other, and we could save money that way. We also wouldn't have to be traveling so much to spend time together," he responded.

"Why would I quit my job, sell my house, and move my 12-year-old son across the country to play house with you?" I asked with conviction.

"But you are my girlfriend," he said.

"That doesn't mean I am off the market! Let me explain it to you like this. You're in real estate, right? When you see a house that you like, and you want to live in it, what's the first thing you must do? Make an offer! Then you must put down a deposit on the house. Then if you're smart, you'll get an inspection on the house while the mortgage company inspects your credit as a borrower, correct? But the thing is, you don't get to live in that house until you do what - sign papers and close the deal. Bottom line, I'm not moving in with you until we're engaged to be married and there is a wedding date set." There was silence for a moment, and then I exclaimed, "When are you going to sell that car?!"

"What?!" he asked confused.

"That 2007 Lexus you bought last year after your divorce. You bought it using the HELOC on the house you two built together that you bought her out of with a five-year interest-only mortgage... in this housing market! And you still have student loan debt! Darryl, you're not living like a man who wants to get married and have children. Financially you're living like a single man without a thought to the future."

We concluded the conversation without any resolution. A few days later, I called him, and he said, "Let me call you right back. Dwight is helping me drop my car off."

When he called me back a little while later, I asked him what he meant about dropping his car off and whether it had broken down. He explained that he'd sold his Lexus at CarMax and paid off the loan. He was also planning for me to meet his mother and for her to meet my parents. We had settled on Memorial Day weekend.

Before that weekend I had made a trip to Chicago to visit my best friend, Cynthia. On the way back, he called me overly excited. He didn't want to tell me why because he had a surprise for me, but eventually, he couldn't hold back anymore and blurted out, "I got it!"

"Got what?" I inquired.

"I got a print of The Doors of Muscatine. I know you said you wouldn't leave Iowa without it, so I found a Catholic high school that was auctioning one off, and I won the auction!"

If I had any questions about his intentions, they were quelled at that moment.

Isaiah and I traveled to Orlando for Memorial Day weekend in 2008. His mother and sister arrived as well and the first meeting with his mother was, well, awkward. We all attended a baby shower for one of Darryl's best friends named Tyrone (Erykah Badu fans will understand how funny that is) and his significant other Linda. That Sunday, my sister drove my parents down to Orlando for the formal Kikuyu meeting. Everyone was polite and got along fine. When my parents eventually left, I was in tears. I knew Darryl's mother had reservations about our union and meeting with my parents was when those concerns would in traditional Kikuyu society be worked out. I could only think that perhaps he had changed his mind about us.

He booked a flight to Muscatine for what we'd named our "Booversary" weekend, which was Father's Day weekend and the summer solstice. He'd planned for us to go to Weed Park, and in great style and with fabulous class, Darryl read a poem to me that he had written.

My Boo
From the first time I laid my eyes on you, I was taken
You made my jaw drop and caused that tingling sensation
Ever since, it has been hard to forget the sight of you,
Who would've ever known that you would become my Boo.
You captured something in me, whether by trying or not,
Your intellect, your words, your presence, you were HOT!
After all this time, you are my dream come true,

How did I get so lucky to have you as my Boo?
When we met wasn't the right time for us to come together,
Today we have something that can handle any weather.
We found each other after some time of being blue,
Now we have each other, I am yours and you are my Boo.
I brought a little something special, a token from me to you.
It comes after four seasons of you and me struggling through.
Something for the Past, Present, and Future, sized just for you,
A pledge from me to always be true to my Boo.
So by this time, I am beginning to genuflect,
I have done all including my initial and final check,
To make sure that I am ready for what I am about to do,
A lifelong commitment...me for you, and for me, my Boo.
I know deep down that this will be an amazing ride,
A life filled with love, with us at each other's side.
I promise that I will do my absolute best,

All you have to do is answer with a "yes" ...
And then he asked me to marry him, and I cried, saying, "Yes!"
We settled on my nephew's birthday, October 9, 2009, as our
wedding date since he was one reason we were brought closer together, and we could share our anniversary with the couple Jerome
and RaeLynn who introduced us. That would give us just over a
year to plan my career change, me and Isaiah's move, the sale of my
property, etc. The merging of two fully functioning households is
a significant undertaking, but I was up for the challenge.

Over the next year, Darryl and I arranged visits with one another, with me keeping track through the spreadsheet. Every time
Darryl had a business trip out west, he would "stop by" the Quad
Cities airport so we could spend face time together. When he
came to Muscatine in August 2008, I remember us debating presi-

dential politics after making love. I had never made love to anyone in that bed before because I wanted to save it for my future husband. I remember us singing the song *True* by Spandau Ballet. We were so in synch, except on politics. Yes, I had met Senator Obama when he came to speak in Muscatine earlier that year, but I still wasn't convinced he should be our next president. We continued to debate naked in that bed, and at some point, he smacked me on the behind and said, "Vote Obama!" and got up to take a shower. I cannot say that changed my mind that day, but I was open to hearing what Obama had to say about healthcare.

We decided to marry in my parents' newly formed Anglican church in Middleburg, FL. Father Hall didn't want to marry us and insisted we do at least three 90-minute pre-marital counseling sessions in person before he would marry us. It had always been a dream of mine to marry in my father's church like my sisters and have him walk me down the aisle with all the bells and whistles. Father Hall made it clear that he didn't want a show. I was spiritually committed to marrying Darryl "'til death do us part!"

At our first session with Father Hall, he told us to take out our checkbooks and our calendars and compare them. What he said was gold, "If you look at how a person spends their money and time, will tell you what their values are."

I had been watching Darryl's money for about a year and had clear access to his calendar, so I had a pretty good picture of who he was as a person. He had the same as me, so I thought he knew all he needed to know about me.

We were both facing termination soon with my declining performance at work due to my health and him facing the end of the space shuttle program. He kept telling me of his coworkers seeking other jobs in increasing droves from his company. I was concerned. He wasn't. He kept telling me about the bonuses he was getting for staying and there would be a huge bonus if he stayed through the last shuttle launch.

At some point in our pre-marital counseling sessions with Father Hall, a pre-nuptial agreement came up. When we got financially naked with each other, Darryl had been floored at the amount of wealth I had accumulated, given we had both studied engineering for six years (he graduated with a BSME from UCF in August 1998) and we both had worked as engineers, he didn't have near as much stashed for retirement as I did even though I had been a single mother. I had no student loan or credit card debt; my mortgage was less than 25% of my take-home pay. I had a car loan that was within reason, stock options that I hadn't exercised, and at least three months of income saved in case of an emergency. We ended up negotiating a pre-nuptial agreement that we hope we never have to exercise.

I went back to Iowa and continued working, attempting to advance my career. I met with a lot of resistance from my White male counterparts. It made working there difficult, and things became even more difficult when my Brazilian friend started dating her now husband. I was isolated, and it affected everything. Once Darryl and I got engaged, we started discussing where we were going to live. His job with the space shuttle program was going to end due to the program ending, and he was having difficulty finding work. I knew it was going to be damn near impossible for me to find work as a chemical or environmental engineer without my degree, so I took a tip from my friend Jerome and read *Purpose Driven Life*.

In the process of reading, I realized I wanted to work in personal finance. Shortly thereafter, I got a job as a financial advisor with Edward Jones. Although I was starting my career in Iowa, they allowed me to transfer to Orlando once we were married. I was only with Edward Jones for a short period, so I didn't make any meaningful or long-lasting connections from that work experience. I did, however, come out with my Series 66 and Series 7 licenses.

While the transition from Iowa to Orlando was challenging, I realized I was going to be building a social network from scratch if I didn't rely on Darryl's well-established network. He'd been living in Orlando since 1992, and it was then 2009. We had our usual wedding shower and the like, all attended by his friends.

With much drama and fanfare, we wed on October 9, 2009, and God willing, neither of us will die before we celebrate our birthaversary week in October with our wedding anniversary and birthdays in one week. In 2024, we will have been 15 married years, and each of us will be 50!

Chapter 5

Part I: Health Wealth: You Gotta Have It

Health! Specifically, good health is a tremendous commodity. To have great health is to be wealthy in a way most people don't consider a priority. That is, until something goes wrong, or challenging or failing health occurs when a person is much older. Health challenges and trauma affect each of us financially as well.

By God's grace, I was a healthy young child. No broken bones. The occasional cold. I had chicken pox when I was small, thanks to a child in the neighborhood. The weird thing about having chicken pox back then is that all the moms would send their kids over so their kids could get it, too and be over with it before school started. Generally, I was healthy. Still, I had signs of anxiety even when I was small. I was notorious for biting my fingers (hangnails especially), even to the point that my fingers would bleed. My parents didn't notice.

According to a pre-natal study from the National Institute of Health, children's health is heavily dependent on the mother. **"A higher risk of emotional and behavioral issues, delays in cognitive development, and even long-term mental**

health illnesses in children are linked to maternal anx‐
iety and depression." This is not a surprise to me as my birth
damn near killed my mother. She was over 43 weeks pregnant
with me when the doctors decided they needed to do a Caesarean
section. Unfortunately, one of the doctors had a hole in his glove,
and my mother ended up with blood poisoning. I ended up in fos‐
ter care as my father needed to care for my three older sisters and
work while my mother recovered. I was in foster care for at least
two and a half months. My foster mother remained in my life as
my babysitter.

I grew up in a dysfunctional Gen X home with a silent gen‐
eration mother and a very African father who came from a very
African, traditional, conservative, foreign household. My mother
wasn't physically affectionate with me after age five or so. The last
time I remember her hugging me in my youth was when I got a
math problem right in first grade. This was because of the genera‐
tional trauma she had endured from her parents, who endured it
from their parents.

After that, there were a lot of beatings. I remember being
about eight years old and being verbally abused for wearing an out‐
fit that she had made for me with a very short skirt and being called
"fast" and a "heifer." I hated my home and used to go downstairs
to my parents' living room to pray at night under the air condi‐
tioning vent. Around that time, I got so miserable that one night,
at eight years old, I decided to run away from home and become
a prostitute to support myself. I packed my suitcase and hid it in
front of the house behind the bushes, then went to bed, planning
to get up in the middle of the night and run away. I would hitch‐
hike onto I-95. Hitchhiking was a thing back then in the '80s. So
were runaways.

Unfortunately, when I fell asleep, I didn't wake up in time, and my mother found the suitcase and beat the Black off me. The physical abuse didn't stop there. There's a picture of me somewhere with my dog Sandy when she was a puppy. You can see the bruise from where my mother had punched me in the face a few days before the photo was taken. I remember changing clothes in the bathroom for a sixth-grade choral performance. A teacher came in and saw all the bruises on my back. She reported it to child services, and while they conducted an interview, I wasn't removed from the home. I would try to run away from home again to get away from the pain and the agony of the tension in my house.

Like I said, the plan was to go into prostitution. The reason I didn't become a prostitute is because I read the book *Go Ask Alice* while I was still young and figured I would just tough it out. The book is about a 15-year-old girl who runs away from home and, in an attempt to soothe her childhood pain through escapism in various means destroys her life. Last year, after sharing the unedited version of this book with my mother, who questioned my memories with complaints about the content, went on to share it with my second sister, who then distributed it to my other sisters. Shortly thereafter, my third sister sent me the book *Mother Hunger*, which helped me understand my relationship with my mother. It also made me more determined than ever to publish this book as it has crippled my family of origin relationships to the point of severe anxiety, added isolation, and more depression.

I was never one to try illegal drugs. One reason is because I grew up in the '80s under former American First Lady Nancy Reagan's "Just Say No To Drugs" campaign and the crack epidemic. Marijuana also had a negative connotation attached to it, so it wasn't something I wanted to try. We lived in an upper-middle-class home, so we had two landlines: the public line listed in the phone book and the private line my parents used. Usually, when that private line rang in the middle of the night, it was a call from Kenya about someone dying. Otherwise, my parents would use it to call downstairs after dinner to tell us to do stuff.

Alcohol was prevalent in my home. I remember making screwdrivers for my father each night and bringing them up the stairs to their bedroom as he read his *Hustler, Penthouse,* and *Playboy* magazines - right next to my mother in bed. Now, I'm not talking about a Phillips or a flathead screwdriver (although he did teach me the basics of mechanics so I wouldn't have to depend on a man). I'm talking about the "get the vodka to orange juice ratio right" kind of screwdriver, and I started making them when I was about eight years old. He would try to cover up the porn with his New York Times and Wall Street Journal, but I remember when I went with my mother to buy those magazines for him one day around that time. We had to go to the bad part of town to get them, and they came in a brown paper bag because we weren't supposed to see the cover.

I asked Mommy, "Why would you buy those for him? Why would you let him look at other women?" I recognized that my mother was obese and not the best-looking thing on the planet.

She said, "Well, it's better than him being out in the street." And from that moment on I was shaken. I felt like it was incredibly disrespectful, and I swore I would never allow myself to be disrespected in such a way.

Things got worse after I started my first menstrual cycle. Picture it: Jacksonville, FL. January 12, 1986. I wasn't feeling great that second weekend, and I spent a better part of Saturday and Sunday playing alone in my room while wearing some hideous homemade clothes my maternal grandmother had sewn for me. They were these horrible yellow culottes with red and blue flowers all over them. Anyway, when I went to the bathroom that Sunday evening, I was pleasantly surprised to see that I had started my first menstrual cycle. Having three older sisters and a mother who was a nurse and midwife, I was already aware of what was happening, and I was excited to become a woman.

I immediately went to my parents' room and knocked on their door to tell them. Maybe it was because I was the youngest of four daughters, or maybe they were just tired because it was Sunday evening, but their response from behind their locked bedroom door was to get a pad from one of my sisters, and my mother would talk to me after school the next day (which she did). That Monday after school, my mother sat me down and had "the talk" with me. She explained to me that I was a woman now and provided instructions on how to take care of myself. What stunned me was my father's reaction to the change.

I had watched my father change his relationship with each of my sisters as they started their cycles, but I believed I was his favorite and didn't believe I would experience what they had. So, when I went out to the garage to hang out with him the following weekend, and he shouted at me to go back into the house with my mother, I was devastated!! It didn't help when, shortly after that, my father broke his silence out of the blue and said to me one day, "All a man is ever going to want from you is sex." I thought that meant sex was all I was worth for a VERY long time.

I asked my mother why my father was behaving the way he was, and she said, "Because he is Kikuyu. You are a woman, and you belong to me now." I didn't know what to think. All my eleven-year-old mind knew was *my father is rejecting me because I can now procreate, and he can't have sex with me which was where my power comes from as a woman.* My father became distant, and even though I sat right next to him at the dinner table every night, he might have said five sentences to me after I started menstruating until I went off to college.

It was enough to spark severe depression in me, and I started acting out. I started drinking alcohol and smoking cigarettes on the school bus with a couple of bad girls. I became a bully. I even bullied my friend Jorge Garcia-Rivera. Years later, after I had forgotten about what I did to him as a tween, I sent him a friend request on Facebook. The following is a summary of the Facebook Messenger exchange between us:

Jorge: Hello Njeri. Are u just trying to boost your friend number because we sure as hell weren't friends growing up? If I can refresh your memory and talk for a second to sixth-grade Njeri. If I recall correctly, you used to torture me on the sixth-grade bus and even sent me home crying after hitting me in the eye. Consequently, this affected me, and I ended up bullying a seventh grader when I was in ninth grade on the bus. He eventually switched schools and died in a drunk driving accident on the turn in Scott Mill Rd right by my street. I only hope he wasn't thinking of me during that tragic turn. Only a few years ago, before he took his last breath right in that same spot, his mom's car pulled up, and she got out. While he stayed in the car crying and embarrassed, she talked to me and pleaded to leave her son alone (which I did). But I know now the long-lasting effects and damage had been done. And I now know that your bullying was the reason I was bullying, not really thinking of it but doing it subconsciously. Kids can be cruel and very fragile. With two kids of my own, I hope I can turn them into confident, compassionate citizens who aren't bullied and don't bully. So anyway, I never got an apology from you...even when you turned up in Stanton later...so I respectfully decline your Facebook friend request.

Me: Dear Jorge, first let me say I am sincerely sorry for the abuse and pain I put you through when we were kids. There is no excuse for what I did to you, and I hope that if you are ever interested in understanding why I did it, you'll let me know. I didn't contact you because I was trying to boost my friend numbers but because I am genuinely interested in how you are doing these days. I have thought of you often over the years and how badly I treated you, never pleased with myself and wondering how it affected you. I know we weren't friends after those incidents, but I do remember us being friends and me going to your house and playing early in sixth grade. I always wanted us to stay friends, but my own situation was why I hurt you. I am sorry to hear that my negative actions led you to do the same to someone else, possibly contributing to another person's demise. I can't express how much I regret what I did and how I feel about the pain I caused you and the following tragedy that resulted from it. I realize now that I didn't apologize to you when I returned to Stanton, and that was my lack of maturity and strength at that time. By God's grace, I have the strength and maturity to do it now, and I hope you'll accept my sincere apology. Finally, I ask your forgiveness as a Christian and hope this will heal the wounds I caused you, both mental and spiritual. I understand you have no desire for us to be friends on Facebook and welcome any more questions or comments you'd like to voice. My ears and heart are open. Respectfully and with Best Wishes, Njeri

We spoke that evening, and I apologized to him again. Then he told me that because of my bullying, he bullied another boy after that. Because of Jorge's bullying, that boy died by suicide.

Jorge: ok...well done. I would be interested to learn why...we all have issues that affect our behavior. I am a student of behavior now with two kids, one being adopted from a foreign country... If I had a chance to apologize to Greg Shrearer, I would take it...so I accept your apology and sorry for calling you or the sixth-grade version of you a bitch...just had to make a point u know ; -).

Me: Dear Jorge, I was abused by my mother and father as a child (who were also abused by their mothers and fathers as children). When I started bullying you, it was shortly after I started being emotionally abused by my father (a long story in and of itself) and had no support from my mother as she physically abused me, much to my embarrassment at R.V. Daniels (there were only a few members of the faculty and one student who knew what was going on with me). I realize now that what I was acting out on you was what I was experiencing at home because of generational abuse. There's no excuse for my or my parents' behavior, but I do understand it. I have made a conscious decision to express the love to my son that I needed from my parents at that delicate time in my life (reasons we do "a hug and a kiss" every time we part from each other and when he goes to bed at night). After many years of pain, I have forgiven my parents for hurting me and doing the best they knew how to do with what they had in their childhoods. I have also come to understand that even though we try to do better by others and our children, sometimes we miss the mark and hurt others... reasons why I asked your forgiveness. Christ came to teach us the ministry of reconciliation, and I would've apologized to you and asked your forgiveness even if you hadn't accepted my "friend" request. It's what I have learned to do. All that being said, if it makes you feel any better, I was bullied every day for a month after school in ninth grade by a group of girls at duPont after I left Stanton. They beat the crap out of me every day after basketball practice, and I never told my mother (I could not talk to my father, whom I had previously been so close to...another long story). I just took the beatings. To this day, I still have a bald patch on the back of my head from those girls ripping my hair out and burning me with chemicals. Anyway, I am truly sorry for the pain I caused you. I hope my request for forgiveness and your granting it has brought *you the peace for which Christ died. With best wishes and warmest regards, Njeri*

Jorge went on to explain that he, too, grew up in a dysfunctional Gen X home and has done his best as a parent to exercise gentle parenting with his kids, which includes an adopted daughter with attachment issues.

While we resolved our issues in December 2008. Jorge and I have not kept in touch, but on August 26, 2023, he accepted my Facebook friend request!

My anxiety and depression got worse when my oldest sister got married and moved out a little over a year later. I literally called her "Mommy" until I was about 10 (everyone called me "Mommy" and my mom "Mommy" as well). It was toward the end of May 1987 when I had my first absence from school. Prior to that, I had perfect attendance from kindergarten through sixth grade (and even got an award for it). I had the stomach flu, which rendered me unable to eat for over three days. I was bedridden and depressed, suffering in her old bedroom. Eventually, after four and a half days of absence from school, my father told my third sister to take me to school at midday in early June. I managed to get back into the groove and finish out the school year. I became an aunt four months later, five days before my 13th birthday. Caring for my nephew became a normal part of my teen routine.

My health wealth really felt the strain from the responsibility of being an aunt when my depression worsened, and I became suicidal at the age of 14. My first suicide attempt was when my nephew was 18 months old. One day after school, I took 16 Sominex sleeping pills and laid down to go to sleep for the final time. I left a handwritten note apologizing to my parents. My mother unexpectedly returned home with my nephew (who was supposed to be at home with his mother). I figured I had better get it together to take care of the kid while my mother cooked dinner. I held him as he slept and while I was crying uncontrollably in front of the television, having a near-nervous breakdown that my parents were oblivious to. Still, that wasn't my last suicide attempt. I figured I hadn't taken enough sleeping pills the first time, so on a drive a week or so later, I asked my third sister to take me to the store to buy more. She refused.

While my other health areas continued to be generally well, my mental health was suffering. I struggled with untreated anxiety and depression throughout my freshman and sophomore years in high school. I was beat up daily for two weeks after school in ninth grade because I had weave in my hair, and the Black girls hated me. I had no friends. I got little support from my family but managed to improve with a change of schools for my junior and senior years.

Leaving home after high school was a significant change for my health. There was no lack of pressure to succeed academically and financially in my family. When my older sisters didn't seem to meet our parents' -especially our father's African-high expectations, I repeatedly heard from my sisters, "You are Daddy's last hope!" Yeah, no pressure there for a child growing up.

Away from home, I finally had control over my own diet and could decide how much to exercise as well as how much and what to eat. I ate like a six-year-old, hot dogs and spaghetti, with sugary cereals for breakfast each day. Instead of putting on weight, I dropped "the freshman 10 pounds" students are known to gain, even though I wasn't eating a healthy and well-balanced diet. Still, I found a new self-confidence as I started attracting the attention of many male students. Because I was 18, I started seeing a gynecologist. Early on, I was diagnosed with dysplasia, a precancerous condition. When I told my mother, she put the fear of God in me. I was terrified that I wouldn't be able to have children, which added to my existing mental health challenges.

Things got to the point that I attempted suicide again when I was 19 over Memorial Day weekend. I totaled my 1987 Mitsubishi Galant, flipping it three times after hitting an overpass column on Interstate 10 at 75 mph. All I could think was that I would leave my parents in a positive position if I died. I was 19. What did I know? When I flipped the car, my neck and spine were compressed, causing chronic neck and back pain, which I will experience for the rest of my life. Seeing a chiropractor was a necessity when I was working in chemical plants due to the physical stress of running up and down the stairs. I was also intrigued by the Eastern approach to health in that it was holistic and incorporated Eastern and non-traditional medicine.

I gravitated toward students and others on campus who were exploring these ideas and lifestyles. I became somewhat obsessed with managing my weight. I ate as little as possible and ran middle-to-long distances (five to six miles) four to five times a week. I had a goal of one day running the Gate Jacksonville 15K River Run. My dad used to take us to the race each year, and the Kenyans always won with what seemed like little effort. I wanted to be one of them (little did I know that they were from a different tribe, the Kalenjin). In the summer of 1994, I got so distracted one Saturday afternoon while running that I nearly passed out. When I finally made it back to my apartment, I was severely dehydrated and vomiting. I called my mother, who instructed me to go to the emergency room. I ended up passing out in the shower and coming back to consciousness thirty to forty-five minutes later. I managed to recover well on my own, but I made a point not to go running long distances like that anymore.

That summer, I made it a goal to get back to my pre-high school weight of 132 pounds. I don't know why I was so obsessed with that number (perhaps because that was five pounds for every inch of my height over five feet), but I only ate a sugary cereal for breakfast, a cheeseburger and French fries for lunch, and some pasta with hot dogs and sauce for dinner. By the end of the summer, I had achieved my goal weight. Ironically, I faced a positive pregnancy test in August of 1994.

I called my mother at work to inform her of my pregnancy after I informed the child's father. She very coolly said, "Well, I am with a patient right now. Can I call you back?"

"Sure," I hesitantly replied.

My mind was racing. Was this real? How could I possibly be pregnant? I had a precancerous condition on my cervix. Even if I was pregnant, my chances of carrying a child full-term were low, given my medical condition. I wasn't sure what to do next. My anxiety went through the roof when the phone started ringing off the hook, with each of my sisters calling to find out if I was playing a prank or really pregnant. I assured them this wasn't something I would joke about. One sister suggested an abortion. That wasn't an option for me as I am pro-life from the womb to the tomb.

I resonated in a state of denial for quite a while. Eventually, my mother asked me to come home for Labor Day weekend, which I did. She, at some point, cornered me in the kitchen and asked me if I was really pregnant or just playing a joke. I assured her that I was pregnant, to which she replied, "Then you better tell your father because I don't keep secrets from my husband." So shortly thereafter, at the family Labor Day barbeque, I said, "I'm pregnant. Can you pass the salad?" to which my father replied, "When are you getting married?" Needless to say, he wasn't pleased when I told him I didn't plan to get married.

Over the next few months, my father didn't speak to me, which didn't help my depression. In late September, I began experiencing severe morning sickness. By early November, the vomiting was to the point that it was contributing to preterm labor. I was hospitalized and given magnesium sulfate to stop the contractions, as well as an intravenous drip to stop the vomiting. Because I was pregnant, I wasn't stressed about medical care costs as I was on Medicaid due to my poverty status. It was my first experience with welfare.

I continued through the winter with preterm labor episodes, but thankfully, the morning sickness ended in late November. I went home for Thanksgiving and, in my emotionally vulnerable and youthful state, allowed my parents to pressure me into marrying my future child's father, even though I wasn't certain I wanted to be married to him. But it was 1994, and I was only 20 years old, and there was still a significant stigma associated with being an unwed mother, never mind an unwed Black mother on welfare.

My appetite improved in the spring of 1995, and I put on almost 27 pounds in four months. While the pre-term labor slowed down, I still ended up delivering my first child almost four weeks early. I was wholly unprepared for the pain of childbirth even though I attended Lamaze classes. In retrospect, the doctors and medical staff took advantage of my youth and doped me up with as much Demerol as they could in an effort to keep me as quiet as possible. Nonetheless, on April 12, 1995, at 9:32 pm, I gave birth to a 6-pound, 8-ounce 21 3/4" healthy baby boy.

I was a natural at breastfeeding and had more breast milk than I knew what to do with it all. I had a bout of mastitis that was extremely painful, and my baby stopped nursing at just three months old because his father gave him solids at three months old. My son didn't want anything else after that. I had a freezer full of breast milk that took almost nine months to use. Thankfully, I didn't need to worry about having enough food for myself and my child because we were receiving WIC (Women, Infants, and Children's Welfare) and food stamps.

In the fall of 1995, I started having significant abdominal pain. I was reluctant to go to the doctor because my Medicaid had ended after my baby was six weeks old, and my parents dropped me from their health insurance when I got married, so I had no healthcare coverage. When my doctor said I needed gallbladder surgery, I sucked it up and figured it out. Imagine being 20 years old and trying to figure out what to do. In November 1995, I had laparoscopic gallbladder removal surgery. That caused significant digestive issues I still manage even now. I faced medical bills that outpaced any income I could even imagine at the time. I started donating plasma to raise money to pay my bills.

Once I started working full-time as a process engineer in 1998, I had a benefits package that was becoming nearly obsolete at that time in the late 1990s. Companies had stopped paying for health insurance for their employees, so I was lucky to have everything paid for by Monsanto in the first year. I had little to no physical health issues for years but found the stress of the job and being a single mother with no support system in a strange state overwhelming. I also had to adapt to what, for me, was a foreign culture. Especially drinking alcohol, which in New Orleans is a big part of the culture.

In the summer of 1998, I started drinking as part of my after-work routine, much like many of the other engineers I worked with. I was a novice in that I had maybe six drinks during college, and five of those were on one night during my first semester in college. After the blackout and hangover from that night, I swore I would never drink brown liquor again. When I started working full-time, at first, it was one or two Bud Light beers with a colleague I had known from my summer internship in St. Louis. Then it became one or two Heinekens with the guy I was dating. Then, it became three or four beers with the guy I was dating. Then, it became one or two beers alone. Then, it easily became a six-pack of beer a day so I could sleep at night. My diet also changed as I slowly incorporated South Louisiana's local cuisine into the foods I ate.

I stayed physically active with a gym membership for weight training and aerobics classes, as well as road running in my free time. I participated in the YMCA Corporate Cup 5K Race each year as a representative of the Monsanto Luling Plant. That event was one highlight for the plant employees' year, so I was happy to participate. That was also a good way for me to improve my business network and social wealth. In 2002, I decided to become certified as an aerobics instructor. I envisioned myself growing a following like Denise Austin or Gilad and being able to leave my job as an engineer. I stayed in pretty good physical health while the struggle with mental challenges continued, even with counseling and medication. At the same time, I was self-medicating with heavy alcohol consumption.

Things were going along fine when, one Sunday afternoon in April 2004, I was playing basketball in the driveway of my home with my oldest son. I reached up to catch a pass from him and heard a pop in my right shoulder, followed by sharp pain. I immediately stopped playing with him and went into the house. Later that evening, I dropped onto my bed with my right arm extended and felt the pain in my shoulder worsen. I awakened in the middle of the night in excruciating pain.

I went to the doctor the next day, and the orthopedic surgeon determined that I had a partial tear of my right labrum. He told me I would need surgery to repair the damage, followed by months of

171

physical therapy. He asked me if there was someone who could assist me with care when I had the surgery. I had no one local.

I reached out to family and friends in Florida and Georgia, but no one offered to come out to assist me. I scheduled my surgery over my son's spring break so I at least wouldn't have to care for him immediately after the surgery while he was with his dad in California. Eventually a male friend who lived in Atlanta, worked as a paramedic, and was sweet on me agreed to help me. The surgery was followed by months of physical therapy. Thanks to the shoulder injury, I stopped teaching aerobics and yoga classes and ended up putting on about ten pounds. I continued seeing a therapist and trying different medications for my anxiety and depression, but more often than not, I medicated myself with alcohol.

I eventually started traveling internationally to help with my mental health. For some reason, going to foreign countries refreshes me, so I started trying to go somewhere new every year. My first trip out of the country as an adult was to New Zealand in October of 2004. I enjoyed it so much that as soon as I got back, I started planning a trip to Italy. Then to Paris. Then, to Norway. Over the course of spring 2005, I realized I needed to move away from New Orleans to improve my career and my mental health. I needed to end the toxic romantic relationship with the guy that I had gone out with for years, and I was finally ready to move on. Things became extremely challenging, however, when Hurricane Katrina hit New Orleans.

I remember when I first moved to Louisiana and realized why the plant was so sensitive to hurricanes. One of the technicians mentioned to me that the city was built below sea level, thus the levees. I was told that if the city was ever hit directly by a strong storm, the city wasn't sure if the levees would hold. The rumor was that if there was a storm, they were going to break the levees on the west bank and let it flood to preserve the city of New Orleans and the French Quarter. I lived on the west bank, and I knew I needed to move because it was just a matter of time before the big storm hit. **I also made sure I had flood insurance when I bought my first home.**

The stress of preparing the plant for the storm was a lot. In all the years I had lived in hurricane-prone locations, I had never evacuated. Even in Louisiana with the back-to-back storms in 2002, I didn't evacuate. I decided to wait until the last possible time after arranging with a girlfriend in Dallas for my son and I to evacuate there. When I woke up early that morning after preparing the house and packing my used car that I wasn't sure was going to be reliable enough to make the drive as it had been overheating, I pulled out onto Highway 90 from my home on Valencia and looked to the east and saw nothing but headlights and looked to the west and saw nothing but taillights. It was bumper-to-bumper traffic all the way to Dallas, so this time, I knew the storm was going to hit.

The added stress post-hurricane of having to work in the area while the city was being rebuilt was outstanding. Like many people, I was pushed to my limits. After just a few weeks back at work at the plant, a group of about 30 of us got together and started gutting the houses of employees who had sustained damage due to the storm. We were told that what we were experiencing was called survivor's guilt and that helping others would be cathartic for us. I spent several weekends for months working on my coworkers' homes. In the spring of 2006, the plant staff insisted that I take a vacation, so I booked a solo trip to Paris to decompress.

That summer, I moved to Muscatine, IA and found the small town peaceful and familiar since I had interned there in the summer of 1997 while I was going through my divorce from my first husband. I made a point to join the local YMCA so that I had a place to go exercise. I tried eating healthily so I could let go of the extra weight I had put on after I stopped teaching exercise classes.

My doctor prescribed Lexapro after an incident in February 2007 with my then 11-year-old son. We got into an argument. I jacked him up against the wall near the fireplace and told him to get out of my house and never come back. The only thought that kept running through my mind was that if he didn't leave, one of us was going to be dead at the end of the week, and I didn't want it to be him. He walked out the front door into the snow, and I stayed inside to cool down. After a short while, I drove over to the local YMCA to exercise to get some of the negative energy out. I looked for my son along the way and inside but didn't see him. I expected him to be home when I returned to our house, but he wasn't there. Shortly after I returned home, I got a call from the mother of one of Isaiah's classmates. Isaiah had walked across town to their house and told them that I had kicked him out. I immediately went there to pick him up. All the way there all I could think was I had to get him to a safe place.

When I returned home with him, I immediately went to my computer and searched for the next flight out of Moline, IL, to Los Angeles, CA. I booked his ticket as an unaccompanied minor, packed his things, called his father, and drove him to the airport. I put him on the plane and drove home in tears. When I got home, I had a drink or two and then called my mother to tell her what happened and what I had done. I confessed my homicidal and suicidal thoughts to her, pouring out my heart. I didn't want to hurt my child.

My ex-husband was furious and dumbfounded when I told him to pick his son up from the airport and that he was on a flight. I didn't dare tell him what had been going through my mind,

174

as he might have used it to gain custody. I had to get help, and fast. I went to the company's Employee Assistance Program and found a doctor who prescribed antidepressants and antianxiety medications. I didn't feel like myself. I felt a need to travel so when I had an invitation to go to Scotland in April 2007, I took it.

That trip was wonderfully therapeutic, but it wasn't enough to fully relieve my depression. I was distracted at work and made major mistakes. I managed to get a better grip on myself over the summer once I started communicating with my current husband, Darryl. Our friendship left me with those old butterfly feelings that I wasn't sure I would feel again after my last relationship ended. We started dating in the summer of 2007, and by the time we were engaged a year later, I was down to my target weight of 142 pounds and felt pretty good about myself.

It wasn't until I started dating my current husband that I was truly motivated to get my diet and exercise habits in order. I had a vision of being the ideal bride (as many women do), and I wanted to be fit so I could be healthy enough to carry and give birth to another child. That fall of 2007 (once we were clear that we were dating each other), I had enough courage to tell him about my family history of mental illness, including my struggles with anxiety and depression. I felt compelled to at the time because my oldest nephew had just been Baker Acted in Florida, which means he was involuntarily committed to a mental institution.

My nephew had threatened suicide after battling depression for years. According to family recollection, sometimes he would take his medication. Sometimes he wouldn't. His family members who lived close by discovered he had ordered a gun online to be delivered to him so he could complete his plan. My second sister (not his mother) called me frantic for advice, not knowing what to do to keep him safe. I made sure he was safe in the hospital and that they would keep him for as long as possible given his history of depression and self-cutting. I then told her to contact the local police department to see if they could work with the delivery service to intercept the gun so he wouldn't have access to it once he was released from the hospital. She said she would try.

I was hopeful when my nephew called me on my birthday that October. He had been released from the hospital 5 days earlier (his 20th birthday) and was on the antidepressant Lexapro. He sounded good. He had a job lined up to start the following Monday and said he was looking forward to meeting my new boyfriend. It was a little out of character for him to say, "I love you, Aunt Njeri," as he did when he got off the phone, but it didn't strike me as clearly until I looked back on it in retrospect. Five days later, my health was forever affected by his health or lack thereof.

That Friday night I got a series of calls that I initially ignored. When I finally took the call, I was stunned by the news of Kaniu's death. He had been found by the police, and his funeral was that coming Friday. Time seemed to stand still for a while.

My first action when I got home after hearing of his death was to go to every picture I could find of him from when he was a baby to the most recent. What I noticed over the years was that he stopped smiling around puberty, much like I did.

My depression worsened after that, and it affected my performance at work. In December 2008, I was put on a performance plan for the second time at Monsanto. I had 30 days to demonstrate my ability or be terminated. Needless to say, the additional stress and not having a boss to protect me left me very vulnerable.

Eventually, my depression affected my work at Monsanto, and I was terminated in January 2009. I stayed at home for a week, awaiting the final severance package meeting. When I saw their offer, I was offended. They only offered three months of severance pay with executive relocation services anywhere in the country as long as I signed a 10-year non-disclosure agreement (NDA). I remember looking at the offer letter and thinking, *"This is all I am worth after everything I've given them?!"* I asked if the offer was negotiable and was told no. I said I felt like I should blow my brains out. All I remember was being escorted out of the plant and the police showing up to question me to see if I was a danger to myself. It was one of the most painful and lowest points of my life.

Unfortunately, the pain in my feet, particularly my left foot (something I inherited from my maternal grandmother and struggled with occasionally), began to become unbearable. It impeded my ability to exercise comfortably. I ended up having a bunionectomy in November 2009. While I went through some physical therapy, my depression worsened throughout that winter, partially from the stress of getting married and moving across the country but even more so from a deep sense of mother hunger.

By the end of February 2010, I was hospitalized after a significant suicide attempt. I was diagnosed with a much more serious chronic mental illness than just anxiety disorder and generalized depression. I had been on Lexapro since February 2007.

After my employment with Monsanto was terminated, one of my sisters came to me with a significant request in the spring of 2009. She and her husband had been having difficulty getting pregnant, and they determined her eggs were part of the problem. Since I was the youngest of four daughters, she came to me and asked me to donate my eggs to her. We'd been here before in my late 20s, but at that time, she wanted me to be a surrogate. I couldn't do it. I couldn't imagine giving birth to a child and not raising it myself. But this was different. I was different.

I agreed to donate my eggs to her and endured all the medical challenges involved in doing so cross country. I had no support system. I had to give myself the shots to stimulate my ovaries. I had no one to talk to really when my emotions went haywire. Never mind, I was trying to do a career pivot, plan a wedding, and make a cross-country move at the same time.

Nonetheless, I managed to produce 16 eggs. The fertility doctor said I was a breeder. She asked me if I wanted to save some of my eggs on ice for myself just in case, and I declined, saying, "I have never had a problem getting pregnant." They got nine embryos from the eggs, and after two implantation attempts, my sister had no successful pregnancies.

I was heartbroken for them. My sister and I had shared a room growing up in Jacksonville and she and her husband were my first-born child's godparents. He had stayed with them for months after Hurricane Katrina hit New Orleans, and he was in Florida for school while I worked to help restore the area and the plant. I wanted to do more, so when she asked me to be a surrogate with my own eggs since she was out of other options, I told her I had to consult my fiancée since it would affect him too. He very flatly told me, "No. The only babies I want coming out of you are mine."

Just five years later, when my husband and I started trying for our own child, I was sent to a fertility doctor after six short months of trying due to my "advanced maternal age." We went to him in March 2014, and he suggested IVF because, lo and behold, I had the exact same fertility issue as my sister, polycystic ovarian syndrome (PCOS). The procedure was going to cost us $20k in 2014 ($26,594.69 in 2024 inflation-adjusted dollars). We weren't prepared to spend that kind of money to have a baby. We decided to wait six months and continue to try on our own after my husband asked me about adoption and I told him that wasn't an option for me.

After I graduated from the University of Florida with my Bachelor of Business Administration degree in August 2014, I grew bored with the free time I had from training for the River Run and studying for school. One Sunday afternoon, while watching an old episode of "The Golden Girls" on the Hallmark Channel, I looked at my husband at the other end of the couch and did my best Blanche Devereaux vixen impression. We spontaneously made love, and then it occurred to me that it was my fertile time.

When my cycle was late the next month, I tried not to get too excited. With my fertility issues, it could easily be a fluke. After a while, I grew more excited and asked my husband in the car one day, "How late would you want me to be before I said anything?" His response was less than positive. That following Saturday, when I was clearly 35 days late, I decided to take a home pregnancy test.

While I was still on an early morning schedule due to school and work, my husband was a night owl who tended to sleep until 12:30 or 1:00 pm on the weekends. It was 10:30 am, but I couldn't wait any longer, so I drove to the local Publix and picked up an EPT (Early Pregnancy Test) double. I could not help my smile as I walked up to the customer service desk to check out. I went straight home and took the test in the guest bathroom. That was probably the longest two minutes of my life! There it was...two lines. I was pregnant at 39 years old!

I didn't know what else to do but to share this incredible news with my husband. It was now 11:30 am. I figured he might as well be awakened now because his sleep habits were going to change in eight months, and this sleeping late thing was going to have to end. I went to our bedroom and sat next to him, sleeping on the edge of the bed. He half-awake said, "Good morning."

I replied, "Good morning!" with an uncontrollable smile on my face. He asked me why I was smiling so much, and I said, "I'm pregnant!"

He rubbed his eyes in disbelief. "What?"

I replied again, "I'm pregnant!" The engineer in him started asking all kinds of questions, like how it happened, blah blah blah. So, I walked out of the room, went to the guest bathroom, retrieved the positive pregnancy test, returned to our bedroom, and handed it to him. After he got over the shock, he was quite excited!

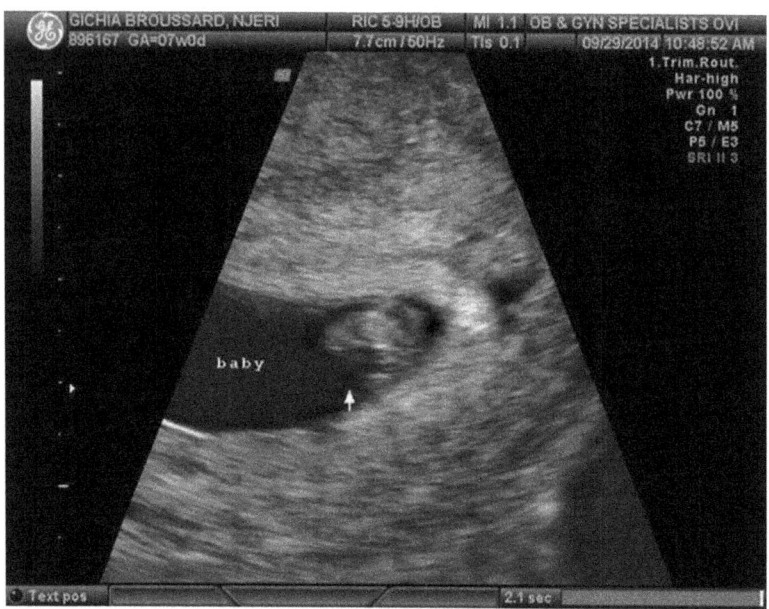

By my 40th birthday, I was far enough along in my pregnancy to announce it to the world. The support I got through my social wealth of Facebook friends was overwhelming. It was through Facebook that I got connected with the Orlando Chapter of Black Moms of Orlando. Several of the women I met through that organization were critical as I adjusted to being at home and working mom again after 20 years. I suffered from some postpartum depression, which complicated things with my psychiatrist.

A year later, while I was working on getting our Jacksonville property management office up and running, my mother called to tell me my father had a heart attack. I went through all the stages of grief, especially when he died the day before Matthew's (son two) first birthday. All I could think was, "Matthew will never know his voice and his accent, all while carrying the Gichia name."

I was already suffering with grief from my father's passing when I somehow injured my left shoulder while working out at the gym in May 2016. I ended up having a left shoulder arthroscopy repair on May 26, 2016. I stayed home and had physical therapy there three days a week for a month while I recovered. This threw a monkey wrench in my plans to get pregnant again as quickly as possible. As the months progressed, I improved, and my shoulder healed. My husband and I continued trying to conceive another child together naturally. In March 2017, we went to a fertility doctor again to find out what our chances of conceiving a second time were. On the day of the appointment, the doctor said I was fertile at that time and we should just go home and try. Ironically, just a few weeks later we discovered we had conceived naturally again! We were ecstatic, especially since we were purchasing a new home for our growing family. Unfortunately, we suffered a miscarriage in May 2017 at an Orlando Mocha Moms event. This pushed me into more of a depressive state, which I tried to manage through alcohol abuse.

After a year of poor self-care, I hit a breaking point in July 2018. One afternoon, it dawned on me that I had been putting my life on hold for someone else for the majority of my life, and I didn't have the one thing I had wanted since I was a small girl: a Master of Business Administration degree. I decided it was time to put myself first. My husband and I agreed that at nearly 44 years old, we weren't thinking of having any more children, and if we did conceive naturally, well, we'd leave everything in God's hands.

Shortly after I was accepted into an MBA program in the fall of 2018, my husband found out that his father had pancreatic cancer. My husband spent as much time with his father as he could, leaving me home with our younger son. At the same time, my husband's aunt, his father's sister, was dying from breast cancer. This put a lot of strain on the family. Things got so stressful for me when, after my husband's aunt's funeral, my youngest son broke his left leg at daycare. Then, two weeks later, my husband's father died. A few weeks after that, my husband, two sons, and I went to Kenya to finalize my own father's burial in his home village of Wanjengi, in Murang'a district, Kenya. That December, I was tipping the scale at 194 pounds, and I wasn't happy with my body.

I decided to take the time I was going to spend in graduate school not just improving my mind but improving my body as well. My intention was to change my diet and exercise routine, incorporating a lot of walking around campus, and let go of 30 to 40 pounds by the time I finished the degree. Imagine my surprise when my 43-year-old self-walked into a program where the average student was 27. I decided I wasn't going to be intimidated and would use their youth to my advantage. It reminded me of something my Great Aunt Leona told me when I was visiting her and my great-grandmother in June of 1992.

I asked great Aunt Leona (who was older than my grandmother) how she stayed looking so young? She replied, "A little bit of alcohol every day. A little bit of Oil of Olay every day. And find out what the kids are doing." I decided to make the best of my time with these young people, including not being outdone during our team-building exercise. That Monday morning, we were all out doing a team-building exercise that included sprinting on a field of leaves. Just five minutes into the activity, I slipped and felt a sharp pain in the back of my left ankle. I tried to get up and walk but was unable. A couple of the other students helped me up, and I hobbled to my car with their assistance. I then drove myself to an urgent care center. There, a doctor did an X-ray and an MRI and determined that I had a partial tear of my left Achilles tendon. It was going to require surgery to repair. That was an unexpected detour for my health wealth while going to graduate school. And the physical therapy was no joke either.

My husband started juicing for me in the mornings, and I started drinking protein drinks increasing the protein in my diet so that I wouldn't be as hungry nor crave sugar as much. This change in my diet helped me let go of a significant amount of weight by the end of that year. In fact, on December 31, 2019, I weighed 174 pounds in total. In January 2020, I started exercising more regularly once my left ankle was fully healed. The weight loss was going well when I started having digestive issues. I started having difficulty keeping food down. It got to the point that autumn that my primary care doctor referred me to a gastroenterologist. That September, I was diagnosed with gastritis.

While at that point, I had reached my target weight of 142 pounds (which is what I weighed when Darryl and I got engaged), I continued to lose weight after the gastritis was resolved, finally bottoming out around 132 pounds. From there, I would waffle between 132 and 138 pounds going forward. Things seemed to be going well, and I was greatly looking forward to my graduate school graduation when we were all hit with the COVID-19 pandemic in 2020.

Being quarantined was an interesting test of my mental health. Watching the stock market plunge and not being sure how people were going to pay their rent when they weren't able to work, and businesses were struggling to be funded and earn revenue? I followed the news like a junkie and helped my husband apply for all federal aid available to us, both professionally and personally, all while completing my MBA. Generally, things were progressing fine until I started working in Corporate America again. I found the stress of working for someone else unsettling. Then things got really interesting.

Chapter 5

Part II

HEALTH WEALTH – SEIZURES AREN'T IT

One afternoon in October 2020, my husband and I went to our neighborhood tennis court for a round of tennis. All I remember was reaching up to serve the ball, and the next thing I knew, I was on a stretcher on the way to the emergency room. My husband told me later that I had a seizure, and he called 911. After a brief stay at the hospital and a review of my medications, the team decided the seizure was a side effect of an antidepressant I was taking. A quick visit with my psychiatrist to change the medication, and we thought everything was fine. I continued managing my weight well with diet and exercise and stayed consistent on my mood medications.

Unfortunately, my husband and I discovered the national drink of Brazil while we were there for our 10th wedding anniversary in October 2019, just before my international immersion class for my MBA. My husband learned how to make them and, during quarantine, managed to practice enough to perfect the drink. We drank them easily four to five nights a week. What we didn't know was how that wasn't going to help things after I had the first seizure. Then, one night in September 2021, I went to sleep in my bedroom as usual and awoke in the middle of the night to my bedroom light on and four White men in the room. I was stunned and confused! My husband got my attention and informed me that I'd had another seizure and that the paramedics were there to help me.

In my confusion, I found myself in a bed wet with my urine. I had lost control of my bladder and needed to go to the bathroom again, so the paramedics helped me to the restroom. They then put me on a stretcher and took me to the hospital for testing. After a couple of days, the doctors didn't find anything, so I was sent home. I remained seizure-free until November 2021. I was taken to the hospital but told the doctors and medical staff that I wanted to go home against medical advice because my health insurance had been canceled by my employer the month prior and hadn't yet been reinstated (financial wealth at its worst, never mind the social wealth of having unsupportive supervisors). At that point, I told my husband that once my health insurance was reinstated, I wanted to get a second opinion because I didn't understand why I was still having seizures with no family history of epilepsy.

That following January, I had another round of seizures and was hospitalized. This time, the doctors made me sign paperwork saying I wouldn't drive until I was seizure-free for six months. I decided the stress of working for the life insurance company wasn't worth it at that point and resigned. My stress level and mood improved immediately when I started working in my own wealth coaching business. I was optimistic that I would remain seizure-free from then on, but I suffered another round of seizures in March 2022.

The neurologist I was seeing put me on Keppra, an antiseizure medication. Unfortunately, before my follow-up visit, I suffered another seizure. I met with my psychiatrist to explore whether the mood medications were affecting my brain and potentially contributing to the seizures. He didn't find anything but reminded me that drinking alcohol was making me more susceptible to seizures. I had another seizure when I went to DC months later for my Tata Njeri's funeral. A month later, on a Sunday evening, I suffered yet another seizure. Terrified, my younger son refused to go to school the next day because he thought I was going to die.

A couple of months later, after my husband came home from dropping our son off at school, I told him I had a problem with alcohol, and I wanted help. I found an Alcoholics Anonymous meeting happening that day, and my husband dropped me off. Once there I got up the courage to share my story. The next thing I knew, I was waking up in the emergency room being asked if I knew who I was, where I was, and if I knew what had happened to me. I was dazed and confused. I collapsed while having a seizure at the meeting.

I was taken aback as there had been no symptoms before the seizure. This time, I decided to take things seriously and try to stop drinking. I met with my psychiatrist, who prescribed medication to help with the habit. I was doing well and thought I would be fine until I had another seizure in February 2023. This time, I decided to work the steps of the AA program, got a sponsor and tried going to 90 meetings in 90 days. I picked up the phone and texted or called someone instead of picking up a drink. I also decided to get a second opinion from a new neurologist. I stopped drinking and was doing fine, but I had another seizure on March 29, 2023. After that, the neurologist suggested I do an in-hospital seizure study, and I agreed. However, thanks to our nation's miserable healthcare

187

system, I couldn't be scheduled until late May 2023 after Memorial Day. I sucked it up, took an increase in the antiseizure medication and took the first available appointment for the study. Things were going along fine including staying sober until I went to visit my mother the first weekend in May 2023.

Before we left my mother's house, I started feeling nauseous to the point of vomiting on an empty stomach. I didn't feel right and slept most of the way home to Orlando. When we got home, I went straight to bed. That afternoon and later that evening, I had two seizures. My husband and I were frustrated, so we called my neurologist the next day and told her about my seizures. I was told it was possibly the stress of visiting my mother that caused the seizures. She called back with the great news of an appointment cancellation and the option for me to move ahead quicker with the study. I jumped at the chance in hopes that she could find a root cause for my seizures.

While sleeping on May 18, 2023, during a hospital-monitored EEG (electroencephalogram), I had yet another seizure. While it wasn't a physical one, doctors did locate the part of my brain that was not functioning properly, and I was diagnosed with left sub temporal epilepsy.

I was put on the highest dosage of Keppra, with a second medication added to hopefully control the seizures. We again thought everything would be fine but were disappointed yet again when I had three seizures on Memorial Day 2023 and ended up back in the hospital. I followed up with my neurologist again, and she suggested changing to a different second antiseizure medication that works on different receptors in the brain since the high dosage of Keppra I was on clearly wasn't working. She said the bad news was I have the kind of epilepsy that isn't easily controlled with medication, so it would take a bit of trial and error to find the right cocktail.

I had been in a similar situation before, as it took almost five years for my psychiatrist to find the right cocktail of psychiatric medications to control my mood and anxiety. Heck, it was 10 years after being diagnosed and placed on different medications before I went without a suicidal thought!

During all of this, I managed to keep my annual OB/GYN wellness visit in March 2023. During that visit, my doctor found a lump in my right breast that didn't seem right. A diagnostic mammogram and ultrasound were ordered. But, with the seizures, I just didn't have time to deal with the new health dilemma. I was too busy dealing with my health insurance company, which made it as difficult as possible to get the seizure medications my neurologist prescribed.

In August of that year, I finally got the mammogram and breast ultrasound. The doctors then told me I needed to have a breast biopsy. Given my generational family history of breast cancer, I wanted to be sure I was well taken care of. The only catch was payment for care was going to be out of pocket. Thankfully, as self-employed business owners, we'd set up a self-directed Healthcare Spending Account years before (thanks to the Affordable Care Act) and contributed to the federal annual maximum.

Unfortunately, Advent Health refused to care for me because I was out-of-network with my health insurance company. I got my husband involved, and he asked them if we brought them cash would they be willing to treat me. They were reluctant. I showed them that we had outstanding bills with their company that were all out-of-pocket, and we were current on all our payment plans. It took a call from the breast specialist for me to be seen, and we worked out a payment plan.

At the same time, I was thankful to reach three months seizure-free. If I could make it to Thanksgiving, I would be allowed to drive again with restrictions. Uber was costing us a ridiculous amount of money for me to get around. Thankfully, I took the extra money we had and threw it at Uber stock as a hobby. In October 2023, I asked my husband if he had an idea of how much we were spending on Uber per month. He said, "$700," and I replied, "Double that."

As a side note, when I tallied up all we spent on Uber in 2023, it came to over $23,000. I'm glad I bought stock in Uber when I signed paperwork agreeing not to drive because the stock is up over 120% as of this writing. What a great example of how financial and health wealth currencies can be exchanged. It's not a stock I plan to get rid of anytime soon.

I did end up having the breast biopsy; it turned out to be mastitis (again), and the lump was removed. This year (2024), when I went in for my annual OB/GYN wellness visit, I updated my doctor on what happened. I told her I had mastitis with my first child over 20 years ago, but I hadn't breastfed my little one for over eight years. What she said to me resonates to this day, **"We don't get to decide what our bodies do."**

As of May 2024, I've been seizure-free long enough to start restricted driving: local roads only and no night driving. Out of an abundance of caution, I haven't driven my son anywhere. If I can make it to Thanksgiving 2024 without a seizure, I'll be able to drive unrestricted.

I am beginning to value my health and my time more than anything else, including financial wealth. I've come to realize that social wealth (close friendships especially) ebb and flow just like the financial markets. I have felt isolated and lonely because of my inability to drive unrestrictedly, which is affecting my mental health during all the challenges of writing this book. I literally feel like I am giving birth to another child.

As I close each chapter in this book, I have come to realize that my spiritual wealth is more important than all five of the wealth currencies I have written about so far. As I also learned early in my adult development, "Success is a journey. Not a destination." (A quote attributed to both Richard Branson and Arthur Ashe.) My associate Anika Allen (a friendship consultant) has added that who is on that journey with you is also important. I hope this book and my next one inspire more reflection on what wealth should look like for us humans going forward, seeking progress instead of perfection.

Chapter 6

TIME WEALTH:
Spending What You Can't Get Back

Astrophysicist Neil Degrass Tyson says, "Time doesn't exist."

Before you get all bent out of shape, allow me to share his full quote for fuller understanding. Tyson explains, "Time doesn't exist. Clocks exist. Time is just an agreed-upon construct. We have taken distance (one rotation of the Earth and one orbit of the Sun), divided it up into segments, and then given those segments labels. While it has its uses, we have been programmed to live our lives by this construct as if it were real. We have confused our shared construct with something that is tangible and thus have become its slave."

If Tyson's opinion is true, is it not possible that we can segment and distribute time according to what our lives need? If so, then it seems to me we can stop allowing time to dictate what our lives need and when it needs it. There would be no consideration for whether you are too old to begin a thing, too young to have a thing, or whether you are running out of time. If Tyson is right, then we can assign new segments and give those segments new labels. Then we don't lack time, nor are we poor of time because it no longer programs us.

In different segments of this book, you likely saw glances of time wealth showing up along the way. I was ahead of my time when I started kindergarten. I was ahead of my time as an elementary student in understanding certain financial principles like saving and spending and insurance matters. I was an older woman in a class of college students and was initially intimidated by that. When I had my second son, I was considered at risk because of my age, and clearly, there was a significant amount of time between the birth of my two sons.

Time is ever-present. Time is there, whether as a segmented clock, a set of pre-determined milestones (like when you get married, graduate from college, or have children), or a principle that you can define and will move when you want it to. Time is one of the most valuable assets one has because once you spend it, you can't get it back and you never know how much of it you have left. It's an Opportunity Cost. An Opportunity Cost is **the potential benefits that a business, an investor, or an individual consumer misses out on when choosing one alternative over another.**

There is a poem called "The Value of Time" by Marlies Cohen. I want to share some of the lines from the poem with you, but when you have a moment, please search for it online and read the whole thing. It powerfully captures the essence of time wealth.

> *"Imagine there is a bank that credits your account each morning with $86,400.*
> *What would you do? Draw out every cent, of course!*
> *Each of us has such a bank. Its name is TIME.*
> *Every morning, it credits you with 86,400 seconds.*
> *Every night it writes off, as lost, whatever of this you have failed to invest to good purpose.*

194

It carries over no balance.
It allows no overdraft.
Each day it opens a new account for you
Each night it burns the remains of the day."

Makes you think, right? Some other lines that will make you sit still and think in this poem are these:

"The clock is running. Make the most of today.
To realize the value of ONE YEAR, ask a student who failed a grade.
To realize the value of ONE MONTH, ask a mother who gave birth to a premature baby.
To realize the value of ONE WEEK, ask the editor of a weekly newspaper.
To realize the value of ONE DAY, ask a daily wage laborer with kids to feed.
To realize the value of ONE HOUR, ask the lovers who are waiting to meet.
To realize the value of ONE MINUTE, ask a person who missed the train."

The poem ends by encouraging us to realize that the present moment is a gift we all have for that present moment. A present valuable asset.

Time can be an asset when it comes to matters like creating financial plans, from budgeting to getting out of debt, saving for a larger purchase, or investing. The construct of time in instances like these becomes your accountability partner. It becomes the gold medal at the end of a race because you agree with time about how it will benefit you. Author Napoleon Hill wrote, "A goal is a dream with a deadline." The goal and dream fueled by your choices and actions create that deadline. The deadline is the point in time you have labeled as your moment of success. Time doesn't say you have two years, five years, 20 years. You do.

Time is also valuable when it comes to honoring and appreciating how we're present and available for ourselves, our vision, our business, our families – especially our children. Any relationship is affected by the number of seconds, minutes, hours, days, months, or years you spend nurturing it. Time is then the gift that you give to something or someone that you value. But, when it comes to different kinds of relationships, time can also feel like you are wearing the weight of the world like a sweater.

Here is what I mean. I spent over two and a half years married to the wrong man. It cost me in every wealth currency that exists, and it took years (time I couldn't get back) for me to finally recover the little financial wealth that came from being married to him. This included me ignoring financial debts I accumulated while married to him, and years of knowledge. That marriage was a horrible partner for anxiety, depression, and being emotionally and physically attacked. Overall, except for the gift of my oldest son, time wealth was exhausted and poorly spent. I was in survival mode instead of finding my hedgehog (referencing the book *Find Your Hedgehog and Stop Working: When You Find Your Passion, Work Stops Being Work* by Socrate and Cassandra Exantus) and health wealth.

I have to say again (in fact, imagine me yelling it): who you choose to marry and/or procreate with is the most important wealth decision you can make. Signing a pre-nuptial agreement with my current husband has allowed me to grow my independent financial wealth based on the financial wealth I had accumulated prior to our marriage. I've heard it said that if you want to be financially wealthy, you must hold on to money long enough to get it pregnant, put it in the money maternity ward, and have it make more money for you. That's what I did with my retirement income, and it has made me a millionaire. Time and choosing a healthier intimate relationship contributed to that.

When it comes to the exchange of social and time wealth, one of the best ways to learn the value of time and how you intentionally use it to serve you is by being a parent. More often than not, children feel most loved when we spend quality time with them. My goal isn't to be a perfect parent. It's to be a parent. My kids feel safe enough to call at 3 am, even if they have done something stupid. I'm THAT mom! My 29-year-old and I had a conversation at 2:30 one morning in which he poured out his heart to me. I'm grateful he feels comfortable coming to me like this, and I pray that I can build the same social wealth through time with my now 9-year-old. Currently, he just wants to watch YouTube videos and play basketball with me. I make it a point to be at every basketball game he has as my health allows.

Once I learned that **"you are the average of the five people you spend the most time with,"** I learned to manage my social/time wealth exchange. I prefer not to be the "smartest person in the room" (which also incorporates knowledge wealth), so I'm often learning and building all my wealth currencies instead of spending my time at a deficit. I have an associate I met through the Orlando Mocha Moms chapter named Anika Allen who has started a friendship consulting business based on this five-people principle. I highly recommend following her.

I also make it a point to **"lift as I climb,"** which is one reason why I offer one hour of free wealth coaching through my wealth coaching business, Lighthouse Wealth Coaching. My mission in my business is to create generational wealth. Giving of your time is one of the most generous things you can do. It's not only tied to social and time wealth but spiritual wealth. This is one reason I'm on the board of directors for the award-winning non-profit organization 8 Cents In A Jar, which teaches financial literacy to eight to 28-year-olds. I also give of my time to Gamma Phi Delta Sorority Inc, Xi Beta chapter which has been a crucial knowledge/social/time wealth exchange.

Something to remember is in 20 years, the only people who are going to care that you worked all that overtime are your family. The question is: will the social wealth legacy you provide be as important to them as the financial wealth?

During premarital counseling with my current husband, the priest said, "If you want to know what a person's values are, ask them to get out their calendar and their checkbook. How they spend their time and their money will tell you what their values are." What value in time and values of yourself do your calendar and checkbook show today?

One way financial, health, and time wealth are exchanged is captured well in this quote: "Being poor now leads to being more poor later. Can't pay to clean your teeth? Next year, pay for a root canal. Can't pay for a new mattress? Next year, pay for back surgery. Can't pay to get that lump checked out? Next year, pay for stage three cancer. Poverty charges interest." Andrew Yang, American businessman.

Yang's point, in some ways, supports Tyson's view of time as a construct. You can take a segment of life and do something with it now. Or you can take that same segment and move it back and back and back only to realize that the ignored construct is now sick, critical, poor, and in danger.

Serial entrepreneur and peak performance specialist Michael Altshuler says something that I believe falls right in the middle of what Tyson, Yang, and I want you to understand, "The bad news is **time flies.** The good news is **you are the pilot.**"

198

As I was writing this chapter, I thought about the MIT study completed in 1972 that used the Long-Term Growth (LTG) model, which predicted global societal collapse by the mid-21st century (around 2040). Recent updates of the study show we as a planet are right on track. Not a fun thing to read as we talk about time wealth, right? But I look at the upcoming decline in population and think about what I heard as a new engineer. Mark Gamel was addressing the Roundup® weedkiller bottleneck at the plant in Louisiana when they said they would hire more engineers to solve the problem. Gamal's response: **"Nine women can't make a baby in a month." The bottom line is some things just take time, no matter how many other wealth currencies you throw at it.**

I believe we're going to see a shift in wealth to those with control over labor and land as we go through the upcoming predicted global society collapse. I strongly suggest you segment more of your time toward learning and investing in real estate. It will be key to continuing generational wealth, as is the continued ability to procreate, i.e., have and raise children to be skilled laborers. Both are going to take time, especially the labor part.

You have to control the time you have and share the quality and quantity of it with those things and people who are valuable to you. The greatest wealth in the world is the love you give yourself; now multiply that and invest in others as kindness.

In closing, I encourage you to read and share **"The Dash Poem" by Linda Ellis**:

"I read of a man who stood to speak at the funeral of a friend.
He referred to the dates on the tombstone from the beginning to the end.
He noted first came the date of the birth and spoke the following date with tears.

But he said what mattered most of all was the dash between the years.

For that dash represents all the time that they spent life on Earth.

And now only those who loved them know what that little line is worth.

For it matters not how much we own, the cars, the house, the cash.

What matters is how we live and love, and how we spend our dash.

So, think about this long and hard. Are there things you'd like to change?

For you never know how much time is left that can still be rearranged.

If we could just slow down enough to consider what's true and real,

And always try to understand the way other people feel.

Be less quick to anger and show appreciation more,

And love the people in our lives like we've never loved before.

If we treat each other with respect and more often wear a smile,

Remembering that this special dash might only last a little while.

So, when your eulogy is being read with your life's actions to rehash,

Would you be proud of the things they say about how you spent your dash?"

It's how I choose to live my life, however much of it is left. Thank you for investing your time in reading my book. May it sow seeds of healing and generational wealth within you and your family and friends.

Suggested Reading

Go Ask Alice by Anonymous

The Speed Of Trust by Stephen M. R. Covey

The Seven Habits Of Highly Effective People by Stephen Covey

Nice Girls Don't Get The Corner Office by Lois P Frankel

The Intelligent Investor by Benjamin Graham

Rich Dad, Poor Dad by Robert Kiyosaki and Sharon Lechter

9 Steps To Financial Freedom by Suze Orman

The Millionaire Next Door by Thomas J. Stanley

How To Avoid H.E.N.R.Y. (High Earner Not Rich Yet) Syndrome by Gideon Drucker

What Would The Rockefellers Do? by Garrett B Gunderson and Michael G Isom

The Power of Zero by David McKnight

Cracking The Corporate Code by Judith L. Turnock and Price M. Cobbs

The Celestine Prophecy by James Redfield

The Da Vinci Code by Dan Brown

Angels & Demons by Dan Brown

The Invitation by Lucy Foley

Facing Mount Kenya by Jomo Kenyatta

The Purpose Driven Life by Rick Warren

The World Is Flat by Thomas L. Friedman

Talking To Strangers by Malcolm Gladwell

Start With Why by Simon Sinek

Our Kind of People by Lawrence Otis Graham

When Breath Becomes Air by Paul Kalanithi

Find Your Hedgehog And Stop Working by Socrate and Cassandra Exantus

Movies To Watch:

Sneakers
Under The Tuscan Sun
The Namesake
Crash
The Bucket List

Music To Listen To

"Dust In The Wind" by Kansas
"Fly Like An Eagle" by Steve Miller Band
"New York Minute" by Don Henley
"Time After Time" by Cyndi Lauper
"Please Forgive Me" by David Gray
"I Need You Now" by Smokie Norful "How To Save A Life"
by The Fray
"Somebody That I Used To Know" by Gotye (feat. Kimbra)
"The Bones" by Maren Morris

www.ingramcontent.com/pod-product-compliance
Lightning Source LLC
Chambersburg PA
CBHW051306120626
46547CB00015B/2118